Making
Backyard Birdhouses

Attracting, Feeding
& Housing Your Favorite Birds

Sandy Cortright & Will Pokriots

Sterling Publishing Co., Inc.
New York

10 9 8 7 6 5 4 3 2 1

First paperback edition published in 1996 by
Sterling Publishing Company, Inc.
387 Park Avenue South, New York, N.Y. 10016
Published in hardcover in 1995 by Sterling
Publishing Company as *Attracting Backyard Birds*
© 1995 by Sandy Cortright & Will Pokriots
Distributed in Canada by Sterling Publishing
% Canadian Manda Group, One Atlantic Avenue, Suite 105
Toronto, Ontario, Canada M6K 3E7
Distributed in Great Britain and Europe by Cassell PLC
Wellington House, 125 Strand, London WC2R 0BB, England
Distributed in Australia by Capricorn Link (Australia) Pty Ltd.
P.O. Box 6651, Baulkham Hills, Business Centre, NSW 2153, Australia
Printed and bound in Hong Kong

Sterling ISBN 0-8069-0892-0 Trade
0-8069-0893-9 Paper

ACKNOWLEDGMENTS

Special thanks to Charles H. Newman for his birding expertise and to Robert Vasconellos for sharing his workshop during the actual construction of the birdhouses found in this book.

DEDICATION FROM WILL POKRIOTS

I dedicate this book to my wife, Mari Jo, for her support, love, and understanding during the time I worked on it.

CONTENTS

INTRODUCTION

Hardly a day goes by when we don't see birds. These magnificent creatures can be found throughout the countryside as well as in city areas.

In spite of the loss of their natural habitats, birds have adjusted to man's presence and have learned to live with him in a world of asphalt and concrete. Man, too, has a basic need to be connected to nature. We can all recall, at one time or another, a memorable occasion when we communed with nature. Often, we find ourselves absentmindedly watching the antics of a bird taking a bath in a puddle or pursuing food. These are the moments most cherished, as we answer our inner call to touch base with nature.

As people become more aware of the delight of bird life around their homes, they find ways to encourage birds to nest and feed by improving the habitat around man-made structures. By planting a variety of trees, shrubs, and flowers and introducing feeders, nesting boxes, or birdhouses and a source of water, you will ensure that birds will flock to this setting and provide many pleasurable hours of bird-watching. Besides the aesthetic value of sight and song, there is the added benefit of the natural insect control these birds provide.

Another bonus is that the environment is being improved because drought-resistant and native species of plants are being planted. Not only will the landscape be healthier, but native species of plants won't require as much water as non-native plants, which will enable you to better utilize sometimes limited water resources.

Even if you aren't a seasoned bird-watcher, providing a hospitable place for birds to live will enable you to witness and appreciate the wonders of nature. And even the busiest person will find bird-watching to be an enriching and relaxing activity.

Birdhouses such as this one are an excellent way to attract birds to your yard.

This setting will prove enticing to birds.

The purpose of this book is to provide you with some simple ideas on how to attract birds to your yard. By knowing the needs of birds and what attracts them, you'll be able to get started quickly. The bird feeders and houses are designed to blend with nature and provide a safe haven for the birds. Before long, bird-watching will become a source of pleasure for you and provide benefits for our feathered friends.

Sandy Cortright

How to Attract Birds to Your Garden

An English garden.

Some species of bird seek cover from predators in trees.

Attracting birds to your backyard or garden can be easy. If you provide for their basic needs of food, water, and shelter, they will flock to it. Increasing the diversity of landscaping will also draw more species.

FOOD

The nutritional requirements for birds vary with each species and with the time of year. First, it is important to know *where* the birds feed. In general, small birds such as bushtits, chickadees, and warblers prefer high, off-the-ground sources where cover from predators is available. A nearby bush or tree can supply a quick escape route from danger. Many other species, which include sparrows, doves, juncos, and larger chicken-size birds like quail, will feed on the ground or on low feeding trays. They, too, like to use a bush pile or low-growing plants as cover when threatened. Humming-birds and other nectar-eating birds will be attracted to hanging nectar feeders.

Birds will include your garden in their territories if natural-food sources such as flowers which provide nectar, plants, shrubs, and trees which produce berries, fruit, nuts, and seeds are available. During the cold months from winter through early spring, birds will find food, especially insects, to be scarce. A bird feeder can make the difference in the survival of both resident and migratory birds.

The nutritional needs of birds are similar to those of

A chickadee in an old feeder.

humans. They need proteins to build and maintain their bodies, fat and carbohydrates to provide energy, and vitamins and minerals to ensure successful reproduction. Being opportunistic feeders, birds will vary their diet if their preferred meal isn't readily available.

Seed preference varies from species to species. The most popular seed mixes include a combination of sunflower seeds (the black-oiled type is best), niger (thistle), millet, peanuts, cracked corn, and safflower seeds. Not all of these seeds will be in every mix. If you have a choice, use a mix comprised mostly of sun-flower, niger, cracked corn, and millet seeds.

In winter and early spring, when insects are scarce, birds such as nuthatches, bushtits, woodpeckers, and wrens will flock to suet feeders to get their needed protein. Blocks of suet can be easily made in your kitchen. (See the recipes in Chapter 4.) A sliced orange or an overripened banana is a high-energy treat for orioles and finches.

(See Chapter 4 for more information about feeding birds and Chapter 5 for information on building feeding stations.)

WATER

A source of water will attract birds to your garden as easily as a magnet attracts metal. Besides drinking the water, birds love to splash and bathe in it, even in cold

Pigeons at a London fountain.

temperatures. Your water source can range in complexity from a simple faucet that drips into a saucer to a commercial birdbath and to an elaborate waterfall and pool. Just hearing the sound of water is a powerful draw to wildlife. Birds aren't particular as to what the source for water looks like. They will drink the water to ensure their survival; the attractiveness of the water source will appeal to the bird-watcher.

Since most birds are "short-legged," they prefer shallow water no more than one to two inches deep. If a pool or stream is deeper than that, a rock or floating piece of wood will provide a safe island. Birds also prefer a rough surface or a narrow rim for a good foothold.

Locate the birdbath away from areas that could harbor predators. Hanging or freestanding birdbaths placed several feet from ground cover are safest. A pedestal birdbath that's three feet high denies snakes and ground-dwelling predators accessibility.

The source of water should be located several feet away from the bird feeder. This will give birds a chance to shake seeds or chaff from their feet before bathing or drinking, thus keeping the water cleaner.

Maintaining a birdbath includes a routine of cleaning it and replenishing the water every few days as needed. Use a stiff brush with soap, and avoid harsh chemicals. Rinse the birdbath thoroughly before refilling. This extra effort on your part will pay off because it will attract many varieties of birds as well as other wildlife. You'll get the added satisfaction of knowing you've provided a healthful, clean resource for our feathered friends.

During the coldest periods of winter in regions where the temperatures drop below freezing (32 degrees Fahrenheit or 0 degrees Celsius), a commercial, thermostatically controlled heater will keep the water from freezing. A word of warning is in order if

A small garden pool.

The basic tools for maintaining birdbaths, feeders, and birdhouses. From far left are garden gloves (to protect hands from droppings, etc.); a scrub brush (for routine cleaning); a spray bottle that contains a solution of one part household bleach to nine parts water (to disinfect any place birds gather); a brush (to remove debris or snow from feeders); and a flexible bottle brush (to clean nectar feeders).

the temperatures fall to below freezing: To prevent birds from getting their feet and feathers wet, which could result in loss of toenails and other injuries, place a plastic-coated wire fence over the birdbath that will permit the birds to drink, but not bathe. A substitute for this fence might be a bushy branch or several sticks laid across the birdbath. Another solution would be to fill the middle of the birdbath with a large object such as a rock or an aluminum pan (upside down) to create an "island," leaving a tiny area to keep feet and feathers

To protect birds from frostbite, which leads to the loss of toes and feet, do the following: When the temperature falls to freezing or near freezing, place a simple barrier of sticks over a birdbath. This will prevent the birds from bathing, but allow space for drinking.

dry while providing a small area for drinking. When the temperatures rise, remove the obstacles so birds can once again bathe.

A glass pie plate inverted in a birdbath creates an island that keeps feet dry, but allows space for drinking.

Nearby bushes and trees give protection to birds when they are threatened. Keep any plants beneath the birdbath low.

COVER

Birds need a secluded place that is removed from the threat of predators and the sun, wind, cold, and rain and provides a safe haven in which to nest and rear young. Landscaping your garden with these needs in mind can attract birds to nest and/or remain as year-round residents. Migrating birds and their offspring have been known to return to hospitable gardens year after year.

Locating trees, plants, and shrubs near feeding areas ensures safety for both the ground feeder and those birds who prefer higher elevations. Varying the types of plants will enhance the look of the yard as well as provide plants preferred by many species. (See Chapter 3 for landscaping information.) Besides plants, trees, and shrubs, brush and rock piles also provide a safe haven

This brush provides safe cover for birds. Note the robin.

Good cover for birds. Note the cardinal.

for rest and nesting. (Brush piles are a favorite of many species.)

With the loss of habitat due to the expansion of urban construction, birds, especially those who seek a cavity for nesting, are hard-pressed to find suitable locations. Birdhouses or nesting boxes can provide safe and suitable housing, and afford humans the opportunity to watch birds and their nesting behaviors. (See Chapter 6 for birdhouse information and Chapter 7 for birdhouse plans.)

2

Seasonal Birding

A migrant bird.

Some birds stay in one place year-round. They have adjusted to the change of seasons and have found ways of surviving both heat and cold and a changing food source. These are referred to as *resident birds*. They can be seen throughout the year in the same general location. During nesting season, these birds may become secretive, and their presence isn't always as apparent. They will, however, reappear as their hatchlings near the fledgling stage (the stage when the young are ready to fly), when feeding hungry mouths is a full-time activity.

Other bird species make annual transitions to different habitats to fulfill their breeding, nesting, and food-source needs. Some birds such as warblers, hummingbirds, buntings, cranes, and orioles fly thousands of miles to warmer climates to avoid harsh winters and then return to their nesting grounds in the springtime. These birds

are called *migrants*.

Other species follow a food source and might endure cold or hot temperatures as long as their dietary needs are met. This change of habitat may only be a few miles away, but at a different altitude, or it could be hundreds of miles away. Birds in transition may stop by for a few days to rest and refuel before continuing on their journey. They are referred to as *visitors* or *transients*.

Which is the best time of day to see birds? For the avid bird-watcher, any time is the best time to observe the comings and goings of birds. Some species are active in the early morning and evening hours, while others seem to come and go throughout the day. Owls, nightjars, and other nocturnal birds can be heard but rarely seen at night.

When the trees shed their leaves in autumn and winter, birds don't have as much cover and they can be more easily spotted. As the leaves begin once again to appear on trees and bushes and foliage increases in the spring, breeding and nesting begins. This cycle repeats itself annually. By checking a birding field guide for your area, you'll be able to find out which species can be seen and where to look for them throughout the year. Whatever the time of day or season, bird-watching will prove an enjoyable and fulfilling way to connect with nature.

A flock of blackbirds stops to rest during migration to a warmer climate.

Landscaping to Attract Birds

An area before landscaping.

An area after landscaping.

Attracting birds to your yard takes a bit of initial work, but the rewards are worth the effort. First, inventory the plants, trees, shrubs, and ground cover growing there now. Do the birds gravitate to or avoid them?

On a sheet of graph paper, draw a plan of your yard. This plan doesn't have to be elaborate or even have exact measurements. There are some commercial computer programs available for the individual who wants to have a precise plan.

When drawing the plan, begin by noting where the windows of your house are and from which areas you can observe the birds. Include all existing plants and lawn. Then list the elements needed to attract birds. By answering the following 12 questions, you'll get an idea of what you'll need to get started:

1. *Is there water available for drinking and bathing?* Birds need a source of shallow, clean water. The sides of the pool should slope and the water shouldn't be more than two inches deep. A simple saucer, commercial birdbath, or fountain or pond would be suitable. (See Chapter 8 for birdbath plans.)

It isn't until the leaves have fallen that abandoned nests can be seen. In the spring, many species of birds will return to the same area and occasionally reuse their old nests.

2. *Does the yard have any mature trees and shrubs?* Birds require cover of plants for protection from the elements and predators. Having an escape route near feeding or bathing areas is essential.

3. *How much lawn do you need?* This will depend on what you want to use the lawn for. If you use yours for a play area or like to mow, by all means keep it. The majority of birds, however, prefer the safety of the cover of plants and seldom venture out to a lawn. Thrushes, blackbirds, wagtails, crows, and doves are exceptions and *do* enjoy this open space. For a good compromise, consider limiting the lawn and expanding the planted flower beds.

4. *Is there a variety of plants?* Gardens with many species of plants will attract a more diverse population of birds. Using a combination of tall trees with gradually lower plants and flowers in your landscape will attract both tree- and ground-dwelling birds. By introducing food-producing plants, you'll get even more visitors.

5. *Where are you most likely to view the birds?* Consider the location of feeders and birdhouses in regard to your viewing areas. Feeders should be in full view for your maximum enjoyment, and birdhouses in more secluded locations.

6. *Is the foundation of the house exposed?* Not only will a house with an exposed foundation lose heat during the cold weather and not protect from heat during warm

These vines cover a blank wall.

weather, the exposed foundation also looks drab and uninviting. By planting shrubs and flowers close to the house, you'll get the benefit of insulation and the opportunity to see birds up close. They'll gravitate to almost any plant, even ones next to your windows. (Consult with a landscape specialist for information on how far plants should be located from the foundation.)

7. *Do you have native species of plants?* As a general rule, these plants are best suited for your climate and will do better than some ornamental species. Check with a garden center or nursery in your area and get advice as to what grows best in your locale. If there's a garden club or native plant society in your community, take advantage of the information it can share.

8. *Are existing plants in the appropriate places?* If a shrub is overgrown and covering a window, it's time to consider heavy pruning or relocating it. Shrubs should be compact and not interfere with your view. Trees planted too close to sidewalks and patios can do damage and actually lift the concrete. In this case, either remove the tree or, if it's a favorite tree, move the walk or patio to a new location or configuration. This is a problem best dealt with by a nurseryman or landscape specialist, who has expertise in this area.

9. *Do you like to, or have time to, garden?* Sometimes we can't spare the time and a low-maintenance garden is best. Removing a lawn and replacing it with gravel, tanbark, or ground cover will save mowing time. Another way to cut labor is to install a sprinkler system and plant-flowering shrubs and limit the number of high-maintenance plants. Self-watering flowerpots will keep color spots maintained with little effort on your part. (Color spots are a bright profusion of color in one particular spot in the garden, as, for example, when you plant daisies in one area.)

10. *Do you have any brush piles, dead tree snags, or wild, overgrown areas in your yard?* For some people, any of these many be considered an eyesore, but to birds they're a treasure. A weed patch, brush pile, or dead tree is a place for birds to find bugs and seeds or to hide, and provides a safe haven for nesting. Some gardeners provide a small secluded corner out of the general view for just this purpose.

11. *Are there changes of elevation on the property?* How you landscape your garden when there's a steep slope or drop-off would be considerably different than landscaping flat land. Proper grading is essential for good drainage.

12. *Where are the utility wires, pipes, wells, etc., located?* Where you locate trees and shrubs might be influenced by these items. Be especially careful about digging near underground utilities.

LANDSCAPE DESIGN IDEAS

For landscape design ideas, look around your neighborhood or town and see how other gardens are landscaped. City parks and botanical gardens are always great places to notice what grows well in your area and how plants look in a garden setting. Observe how tall and wide some trees and shrubs are and how closely together they grow. Ask experts how long it takes for plants to reach maturity and how much care is needed. You might want to consider purchasing larger, mature trees rather than wait ten years for seedlings to grow to the desired size.

Note how tall plants are usually placed in the background near a fence, and shorter ones are planted in front of them. If you do this, a garden can have a gradual progression of plants that starts with tall ones in back and ends with low flowers towards the middle of the yard.

Whether you're landscaping a large estate or a ten-

A botanical garden in Oxford, England.

foot-square patch of land, the same principles should be applied. Look from your window and decide what kind of background your view should have. Do you want to screen a bare fence or an unattractive garage? Or maybe you'd like some privacy from the street or neighboring homes. If you want instant privacy while you're waiting for the hedge or trees to grow, consider a temporary trellis with quick-growing vines.

Start with grading and proper drainage, and then plant the large trees and shrubs. The fences could be added at this time, too. As time and money permit, fill in the rest of the garden over a period of time. Break

Short plants are in front, and tall plants in back.

the landscaping projects down into a reasonable time schedule. Good gardens don't happen overnight; sometimes it takes many years of growth to produce the type of garden you want. The birds will still come in spite of a lack of perfection.

Besides plants, a fountain, pool, sculpture, rock walls, individual large rocks, or color spots can draw your eyes to the garden. An ornamental bird feeder or birdbath would make a wonderful main point of interest. Soften the corners of the house by placing rounded shrubs there. Gardens with curving, uneven edges are more pleasing to the eye and much easier to maintain. Use tall, dense shrubs to screen off an undesirable view.

A magpie visits an English garden.

This small garden in York, England, provides an area for birds.

A small garden in Edinburgh, Scotland.

WHAT KINDS OF PLANTS ARE BEST?

Since there are as many different types of climates as there are birds, it is almost impossible to specify exactly what to plant. You can, however, get this information from your local nursery, garden center, or native plant society. Probably the easiest source, however, would be fellow gardeners, especially those who have landscaped to attract birds to their yards. Also, government agencies often have publications with suggestions covering plants best suited for your locality.

Trees, shrubs, and plants that produce fruit or seeds are a good choice. Conifers produce seed cones and are drought-resistant. Flowers that make lots of nectar are also great if hummingbirds or orioles come into your area. Perennials and annuals are also a wonderful source of nectar when in blossom; after these plants have bloomed, their seeds will provide a source of food. Berries, fruit trees, and seed-producing flowers such as sunflowers are a great asset to any yard. Try planting vegetables among the flowers. Corn looks great and it grows fast. The stalks could be put on the brush pile, too. Herbs can be introduced into gardens and harvested as needed. Plant melons and save the

Ampelopsis brevipedunculata (*Porcelain berry*).

Dioscorea batatus (*Common vine*).

seeds for the birds in winter. Introduce oats, barley, or wheat in a small patch to supply the birds with food in winter.

Utilize cacti and other plants that have adapted to harsh environments in dry, arid climates. Use rocks and a dripping waterfall to create an oasis for migratory species. Birds will flock to a spot of greenery, and if there's shade, cover for safety, and a source of food, they may stay and become residents.

HUMMINGBIRD GARDEN

Hummingbirds are found only in the Western Hemisphere and are considered tropical birds. Of the 320 species found in North and South America, only 16 are found north of the Mexican border. The highest concentration of hummingbird species can be found in Ecuador, with 163 recorded.

For those people who are fortunate enough to have resident hummingbirds or other nectar-eating birds, knowing what to plant in the garden is important. Start with a trip to a nursery to see which nectar-producing plants are available and grow well in your area. Hummingbirds will feed from over 100 different flowering plants. Included are petunias, impatiens, salvia, agapanthus, honeysuckles, mints, flowering fruit trees,

Good landscaping for a dry climate.

and thistle. Hummingbirds also supplement their diet with small insects and spiders, which provide needed protein.

It has been observed that hummingbirds seldom use a birdbath, but will take advantage of misters and rising water vapors for bathing and possibly for drinking. (A mister is a device with a sprinkler head that will break water down into smaller droplets.) Their nesting sites are usually near a source of water which has plant cover.

Placing feeders with a nectar comprised of one part sugar and four parts water will bring hummingbirds to feed. Adding more sugar is detrimental to the birds, while less than a one to four ratio of sugar to water will

A low-maintenance cactus garden.

not give the needed energy required. Honey is *not* recommended as a sugar substitute because it cultures fungi.

It's essential to keep feeders free from bacteria and fungus by cleaning them on a regular basis or at the time of refilling. If there is any red coloring or decoration on the feeder, red food coloring added to the sugar water is unnecessary.

This large brush pile provides a home for wildlife.

Hummingbirds are attracted to red.

Leave a place for a dust bath.

BRUSH PILES

At first glance a brush pile looks similar to a messy haystack, but to many birds it provides a safe haven and ideal nesting place. Ground-nesting birds such as quail, pheasant, and grouse find safety from predators and insulation from the elements in the thick layers of branches. Brush piles are also used by a variety of wildlife, including possums, rabbits, lizards, snakes, and any number of rodents. Smaller birds will take

advantage of the higher branches. In the large garden, this is an ideal way to create a sanctuary. If brush piles are placed at the side of a house or in an area that has tall plants to screen it from view, they will serve as a place to store debris and not be an eyesore for the neighbors to complain about.

An alternative to the large sprawling brush pile is the smaller version shown on page 24. By placing branches inside the three guide poles, the same safe cover is created in a tidy manner. Vines can be grown that will use the branches to climb on. This structure can be placed in a prominent location in any garden. Not only will wildlife take advantage of the cover it provides, but small birds will choose it as a site for nesting.

A tidy brush pile for a small garden.

Feeding Birds

A simple doughnut feeder can be made by placing a plastic cup on string or yarn. Push a doughnut into the cup and hang the cup where squirrels can't reach it. The best doughnuts are the cheap, greasy ones. (Stale doughnuts are good, too.) Push sunflower seeds into the doughnut to attract birds to the doughnut.

A bird must find and eat incredible amounts of food to survive. Each day a tiny hummingbird must consume an amount of nectar equivalent to its weight to maintain its high metabolism; other species, to a lesser degree, must find enough protein for energy to fuel their bodies so they can pursue their many activities.

When planning a bird-feeding area, keep in mind the kinds of bird you'd like to attract. Some feed from elevated trays, while others prefer eating off the ground. Nectar eaters will need hanging feeders. A combination of feeders will bring the most diverse bird population to your garden.

During cold weather, birds need an extra source of energy such as suet. This hard beef fat is easily rendered and can be mixed with a combination of seeds and dried fruit for a hardy fare. Birds will seek this food source during any time of year, but winter is when it's

Give the ground-feeding birds a winter banquet by placing a tray of their favorite foods on the ground. Include orange slices, berries, seeds, and suet. Note the food preferences of different species.

Suet in a net bag.

A plain titmouse eating suet.

Suet in a hardware cloth holder.

most valuable. You can alter the following recipes by adding or omitting ingredients. By noting what food-stuffs the birds eat first, and what is left for last, you can cater to their preferences.

SUET CAKES

Suet is the term referring to the white fat from beef. This can be obtained inexpensively or sometimes for free from a butcher. To *render* means to melt the fat down. Grind or chop the fat into small pieces to expedite the rendering process. Rendering can be done by any one of the following methods.

Stove-Top Method

Place the suet in a heavy pan or double boiler and cook it over a medium heat until it bubbles. Then add ½ inch of water. Cover the suet and lower the temperature to low heat. Stir as needed. This is a slow method, but one that requires little attention.

Microwave-Oven Method

This is a quick, easy method that demands constant attention. Place the suet in a microwave and cook it in a covered dish at medium power.

Oven Method

Place the suet in a large, covered baking dish and cook it at 350 degrees Fahrenheit (177 degrees Celsius) until it melts. Stir it occasionally. This might take several hours, depending on the volume of fat.

After the fat has melted away from the cracklings, sieve it, and then refrigerate it for up to two weeks. Frozen suet can be kept for months. A pound of suet will yield about a pint of fat. The cracklings are a welcome snack for birds, especially in cold weather.

Recipes

The following recipes can be altered by adding flour, cornmeal, cut-up dried fruit, shredded coconut, cooked rice, sugar, dried peas and beans, or any combination of seeds. Try substituting ingredients such as lard for suet or cornflakes for rolled oats. Experiment and see what preferences the birds have.

Suet Cake Recipe #1

Mix together:
1 cup of melted suet
½ cup of peanut butter (crunchy or plain)
1 cup of sunflower seeds or birdseed mix

Pour the mixture into muffin tins or small plastic dishes. Refrigerate until it is solid. When the suet cake is ready to use, place in a suet holder or basket or in a plastic net bag such as used for produce. These bags can be suspended from eaves or branches and away from squirrels.

Suet Cake Recipe #2

Mix together:
1 cup of melted suet
½ cup of rolled oats
½ cup of raisins or peanuts
½ cup of cornmeal
½ cup of sunflower or other seeds

Pour the mixture into muffin tins or plastic dishes. Refrigerate until it is solid. Keep the suet cake in the refrigerator or freezer until it is ready to use. Then place it in a suet feeder or net bag.

SEED PREFERENCES

Birds, just like people, have food preferences and, when that source runs out, will settle for something else. As the seasons change, the availability of seeds, insects, nectar, and fruit will fluctuate. Being opportunistic feeders, birds will take advantage of whatever is readily available in the immediate area or fly on to greener pastures. For those birds that don't migrate, a feeder is their main food source.

Try this experiment: Put several shallow dishes or pie tins on a table and place a different kind of birdseed in each. Include white and red millet, sunflower seeds, cracked corn, canary seed, niger (thistle), peanut hearts, oat groats, and wheat. These are the most popular birdseeds. Observe which seed is chosen by different species. You can buy individual mixtures of seeds in bulk at pet, seed, or wild-bird stores or you can try mixing your own.

When you've found which birdseeds are preferred, buy a mix high in those seeds. Many commercially packaged cheap seed mixes are mostly made up of the least-desirable seeds such as milo. If the birds do not like the offering, they'll search for other sources before they'll eat from your feeder.

Before putting seed out on the feeder, place it in the microwave oven for 3½ minutes on high to sterilize it. This way, if the seed falls on the ground it won't sprout.

Certain "people" foods such as popped corn, fruit (both fresh and dried), cereals, nuts, scrambled eggs, doughnuts, meat scraps, lard, bacon drippings, and table scraps are suitable for feeders. Birds have also been known to raid cat- and dog-food dishes for an easy meal. Sometimes it's not the food, but the insects the food scraps attract that the birds come for. If the temperature is warm, these foods should be removed within a day if not eaten.

During nesting season, females need extra calcium in their diet. You can feed them chicken eggshells if you wash the shells and then dry them in the oven. Shells will crumble easily. Place them on the feeder with the seed mix. Another source of calcium and grit is crushed oyster and clam shells. Up to 10% of your seed mix can be comprised of eggshells. This type of seed mix can be purchased at a feed store.

A pinecone feeder.

FEEDERS

Pinecone Feeders

Pinecones contain small nut meats and are ready-made food containers. To make a pinecone feeder, do the following:

1. Wrap a wire or string to the stem end of the cone if it will be used on a wreath, or tie it to the pointy end to create a hanging feeder.

2. Stuff chunks of raw suet in the crevices or spaces of the cone.

3. Holding the wire or string, dip the cone into melted suet and then immediately roll it in birdseed. The result is a seed-encrusted feeder which can be hung from a branch. Smaller cones can be attached to a wreath made of branches bearing berries or seed pods. Hang it on a fence and watch the birds devour the goodies.

Use a strong hanger to hang feeders and birdhouses. Protect the tree with foam pad.

Nectar Feeders

Hummingbirds and orioles love to eat nectar from feeders. Bring to a boil a mixture of two cups water and ½ cup sugar. (Do not increase the sugar content of this recipe. This can harm birds.) Let the mixture cool uncovered; then store it in the refrigerator until needed. Some people add food coloring to attract the birds. This isn't necessary if your feeder has red on it. Plastic flowers, ribbons, or red paint will attract hummingbirds. Be sure to monitor the feeder and clean it before every refilling. Honey is *not* recommended as a substitute for sugar because it can ferment easily and harmful fungus can grow quickly.

Locating Feeders

Where are you most likely to watch the birds? People watch from the dining area, living room, bedroom, front porch, patio, or kitchen. No matter what your preference is, place your feeder or feeders so they can be easily seen. Having a tree or shrub to use as cover nearby will encourage birds to flock to the feeder. They can use a branch as a waiting place while other birds are eating.

Don't be discouraged if it takes a few days or even weeks for birds to come to a new feeder. When the

Birds like a nearby perch.

food source is discovered, you'll have a steady stream of customers.

Care of Feeders

Periodically clean the feeder by brushing it off and removing any spoiled food and/or droppings. In the winter, it's important to remove snow so the birds can have access to their food.

DEALING WITH CATS

Is it possible to find a way for birds and cats to coexist? It's estimated that an outdoor cat will kill as many as 50 birds a year. By nature, cats are hunters, and birds are a mighty tempting meal just ready to be plucked from a nest or from under a bird feeder. On the other hand, cat owners have a responsibility to control their pets, which means keeping them out of your garden.

There's no easy way to solve this dilemma. However, by trying to outmaneuver the cat, you might find a solution everyone can live with. Here are some suggested ways to discourage cat predation:

1. Use only pole-mounted nesting boxes. Metal poles or posts with a metal funnel guard or wrapped with metal will discourage climbing. For rectangular feeders, attaching 16-inch Plexiglas that hangs below the feeder base on all sides will discourage access from below. Metal guards could also be attached to trees where nests are built. (See Chapter 5 for plans.)

2. Use a metal cage beneath pole-mounted feeders to protect ground-feeding birds. (See Chapter 5 for a plan.)

3. Check with animal-control specialists in your community. They can give you advice on how to trap feral cats and dispose of them in a humane manner.

4. Place feeders away from any ground cover cats could use for hiding, or fence off the cover to prohibit ambushes. Mow any high grass within six feet of the feeder.

5. Implore cat owners to keep their pet indoors, or to limit its access to the outdoors. Ask the owners to keep the cat well-fed so it won't need to hunt for food. Placing a bell on the cat's collar is only of marginal help because birds don't relate the tinkling sound to danger.

A cat fence.

If you still have problems, trap the cat and return it to its owner. Be firm, and tell the owner that if his/her cat gets caught again, they will have to retrieve it from the animal control or Humane Society pound.

DISCOURAGING SQUIRRELS AND OTHER WILDLIFE

For those who have squirrels with a penchant for raiding feeding stations, a bit of strategy can thwart them. Ground feeding trays can be covered with wire fences which will let small birds, but not squirrels, enter. (See Chapter 5 for plan.) Pole-mounted feeders that are equipped with a metal cone or cylinder-shaped collar will deter entry from below the feeder. Remember, squirrels are capable of long jumps. Locate collars four to five feet above the ground. The feeder post should

Squirrels can be pesky creatures.

be eight feet away from any object like a fence, tree, or building. Use metal or slippery-surface poles to discourage climbing. For hanging feeders, a dome-shaped roof collar will discourage entry from above. Another alternative is to place food for squirrels (corn, sunflower seeds, etc.) far away from the bird feeder so they'll hopefully be satisfied and not covet bird food.

As the urban sprawl reaches further into what was once the undisputed territory of creatures such as raccoons, skunks, possums, rats, and snakes, we must be aware they are around us and have adjusted to us by scavenging from our gardens. They come at night under the cover of darkness to raid bird nests and eat food from feeders. Just as it is in the wild, part of the diet of these animals is bird eggs, small hatchlings,

This squirrel has no problems climbing a pole.

The screened feeding area under the pole-mounted feeder keeps squirrels, raccoons, and larger birds from enjoying the food dropped by small birds.

seeds, fruit, nuts, and just about any other food humans consume.

To discourage these animals, refer to the section on "Dealing with Cats" on page 30.

This squirrel guard is a flat disc.

DEALING WITH "GREEDY" BIRDS

Sometimes you'll get more than your share of a particular species of bird such as pigeons or doves that consumes everything in sight. An easy way to screen them out is to put a protective wire covering over the feeding area. (See Chapter 5 for plan.) Little birds can get in, and the big ones stay out. Another way is to make the cover or roof of the feeder too low for the big ones to get access to the food. They'll be content to eat the spilled seed on the ground under the feeder. Maybe sparrows are the birds you'd like to discourage. In this case, consider a hanging feeder, which sparrows don't

like, and fill it with seeds other than cracked corn.

If a flock of starlings or other undesirable birds descends on your garden, remove the food from the feeder and in a couple of days they'll move on. Finches and other songbirds usually return immediately when food is reintroduced.

Only small birds are welcome.

A 1-inch hardware cloth cage protects seedlings.

5

Feeding Station Plans

There are four basic aspects to building a bird feeder. They are as follow:

1. *Decide on what kind of birds you'd like to attract and feed.* If you want to exclude large birds, make the roof close to the floor of the feeder or use chicken wire or wire mesh to keep larger birds out. For ground feeders, a wire cage works well.

2. *Build a properly designed feeder with sturdy materials.* This type of feeder will protect the seeds from rain, snow, and wind and keep them dry. If moisture does get under the roof line, adequate drainage is essential.

3. *The feeder should have some provision for easy cleaning.*

4. *Decide on where to place the feeder in the yard.* Proper placement is critical for the protection of the birds from predators and to keep food thieves away. Consider which areas are best for your viewing enjoyment too.

CRIMSON DELIGHT MATERIALS LIST

Wood
½″-Thick Exterior Plywood

Number of Pieces	Diameter	Diameter of Hole	Part
1	4⅜″	No Hole	Top
1	4⅜″	1¼″	Bottom

Hardwood Dowels

Quantity	Diameter	Length	Part
3	⅜″	9⅞″	Sides

Miscellaneous Materials
Galvanized Wire

Quantity	Diameter	Length	Part
3	15 gauge	4″	Top Supports
3	15 gauge	1″	Wire Keys

Stainless-Steel Key Ring

Quantity	Diameter	Finish
1	1″	Stainless Steel

Glass Tubing

Quantity	Diameter	Length	Part
1	¼″	3″	Feeder Tube

One-Hole Stopper

Quantity	Diameter	Length	Part
1	¾″	1″	Stopper

Plastic Calistoga Bottle

Quantity	Diameter	Length
1	2¾″	8⅞″

INSTRUCTIONS*

1. Lay out the top and the bottom parts of the plywood.

2. Cut the dowels to size.

3. Drill all holes in the plywood and the dowels.

4. Cut out the round pieces for the top and bottom parts.

5. Bend the top support wires so that there is an eye at one end and a slight hook at the other. Make sure that all three are the same length and shape. Now, attach the eyes to the key ring. The other ends will go in the dowels later.

6. Put the dowels in place on the bottom part. Secure them with the short 1″-long wire keys. (Bend the wire keys to an S shape.)

7. Place the bottle in the assembly and put on the top piece.

8. Attach the top support wires to the dowels. You may have to bend them slightly to align them correctly.

9. Once all the parts are fitted properly, remove the bottle and then prime and paint the parts a bright red.

10. Heat the center of a glass tube over a flame to make a 100° bend halfway. The glass will bend when it turns a yellowish color. Be careful to use proper tools such as tongs to hold the glass as you heat it.

11. After letting the glass cool, insert the glass into the stopper.

12. Fill the bottle with a solution of water and sugar. Add red food coloring to make the solution colorful.

*If using another type of bottle, modify the plans to fit yours.

Crimson Delight feeder for nectar-feeding birds such as hummingbirds.

Drawing of Crimson Delight feeder.
Also see following page.

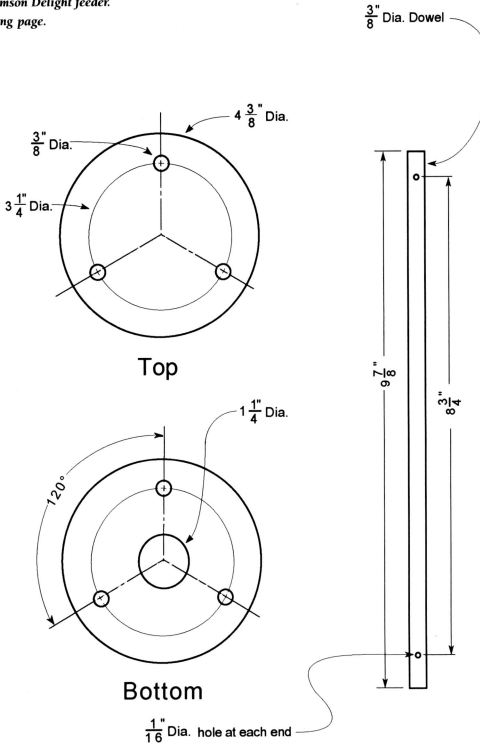

$\frac{3}{8}$" Dia. Dowel

$4\frac{3}{8}$" Dia.

$\frac{3}{8}$" Dia.

$3\frac{1}{4}$" Dia.

Top

$1\frac{1}{4}$" Dia.

120°

Bottom

$9\frac{7}{8}$"

$8\frac{3}{4}$"

$\frac{1}{16}$" Dia. hole at each end

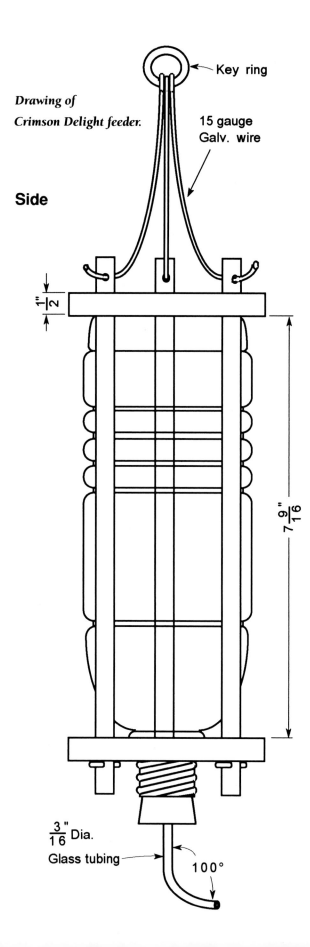

Side

*Drawing of
Crimson Delight feeder.*

Key ring

15 gauge
Galv. wire

$\frac{1}{2}$"

$7\frac{9}{16}$"

$\frac{3}{16}$" Dia.
Glass tubing

100°

DAS GRÜNE HAUS
MATERIALS LIST

Wood
Any ¾"-Thick Redwood, Cedar, etc.

Number of Pieces	Width	Length	Part
1	7¾"	7¾"	Back
1	5¾"	10¾"	Top
1	2"	9¼"	Front
2	5½"	7¾"	Sides
1	4¾"	7¾"	Base

Miscellaneous Materials
Galvanized Nails

Quantity	Size	Length
½ lb.	5d	1¾"

INSTRUCTIONS

1. Lay out all parts on the wood.

2. Cut out all parts.

3. Assemble the base to the back with glue and nails.

4. Attach the sides to the back and base by gluing and nailing them together.

5. Secure the front to the sides and base using glue and nails.

6. Attach the top to the assembly with glue and nails.

7. Finish the feeding station with primer and green paint. *When painting the outside of any project, use non-toxic water-based exterior paint.*

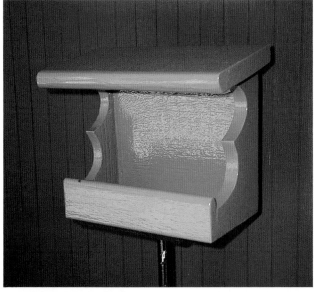

Das Grüne Haus *feeder.*

Drawing of **Das Grüne Haus** *feeder.*

$\frac{1}{2}$" Squares

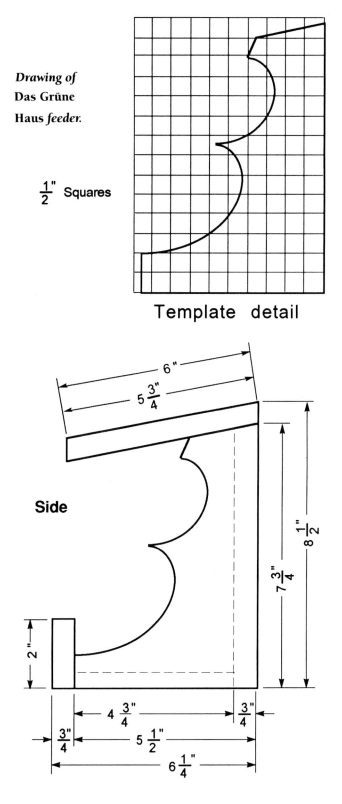

Template detail

Side

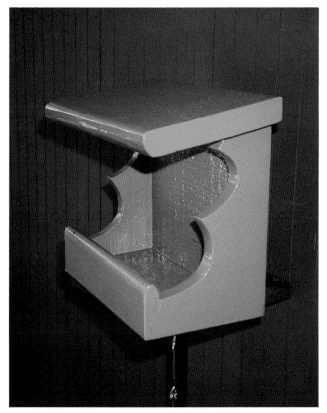

Another view of **Das Grüne Haus** *feeder.*

Drawing of
Das Grüne Haus *feeder.*

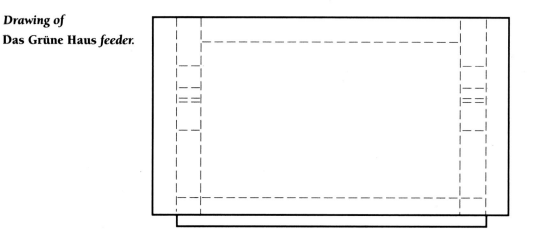

Top

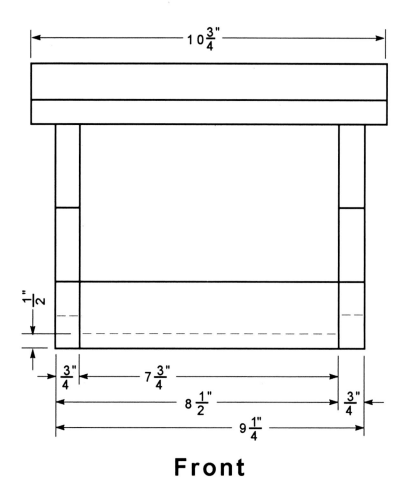

Front

FEATHERED FRIENDS EATERY MATERIALS LIST

Wood Bowl 6" in Diameter and 2" Deep

Aluminum Sheet

Quantity	Diameter	Gauge Size	Part
1	11"	16 to 12	Guard

Lamp Rod

Quantity	Diameter	Length	Finish
1	⅜"	10"–12"	Chrome

Lamp Rod Nuts

Quantity	Diameter		Finish
3	⅜"		Chrome

Lamp Rod Threaded Eye

Quantity	Diameter		Finish
1	⅜"		Chrome

Flathead Aluminum Rivets

Quantity	Diameter	Length	Finish
3	¹⁄₁₆"	¼"	Aluminum

INSTRUCTIONS

1. Lay out the guard on the aluminum sheet. If you are using a guard with a fluted top, make a full-sized pattern and place it on the aluminum sheet at the correct angles.

2. Drill the three ¹⁄₁₆" rivet holes and the ⅜" hole in the middle of the bowl.

3. Cut the guard to size. File or sand any rough edges.

4. Form the guard over a rounded object such as a baseball bat or a large pipe.

5. Rivet the ends of the guard together.

6. Redrill the ⅜" hole in the top of the guard from the inside.

7. Mount the bowl on the rod with two nuts. Then place the other nut on the top of the guard, place the guard on the rod, and add the threaded eye.

Feathered Friends Eatery.

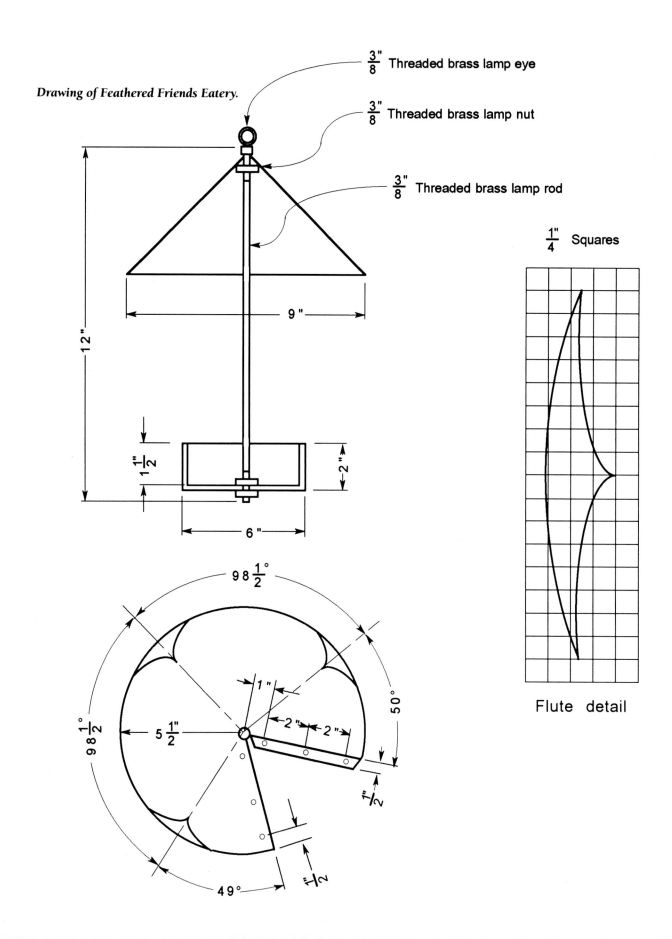

$\frac{3"}{8}$ Threaded brass lamp eye

$\frac{3"}{8}$ Threaded brass lamp nut

$\frac{3"}{8}$ Threaded brass lamp rod

Drawing of Feathered Friends Eatery.

12"

9 "

$1\frac{1"}{2}$

2 "

6 "

$98\frac{1}{2}°$

$98\frac{1}{2}°$

50°

49°

$5\frac{1"}{2}$

1 "

2 " 2 "

$\frac{1}{2}"$

$\frac{1}{2}"$

$\frac{1"}{4}$ Squares

Flute detail

HOMESTEAD WINDOW FEEDER MATERIALS LIST

Wood

Any ¾″-Thick Redwood, Cedar, etc.

Number of Pieces	Width	Length	Part
1	9½″	37½″	Back
1	8″	36″	Top
1	7½″	37½″	Front
2	8″	7½″	Sides
1	8″	6″	Center Brace
1	2″	8″	Divider Block

Miscellaneous Materials

Nails

Quantity	Size	Length	Finish
½ lb.	5d	1¾″	Galvanized

INSTRUCTIONS

1. Lay out all parts on the wood.

2. Cut out all parts.

3. Drill a pilot hole for a jigsaw or sabre saw, and cut the 6″-diameter pot hole.

4. Assemble the sides to the back with glue and nails.

5. Attach the top to the back and sides with glue and nails.

6. Glue and nail on the divider block.

7. Secure the front to the sides, top, center brace, and divider block using glue and nails.

8. Decorate the front with cattle brands using a wood-burning tool.

Homestead feeder.

Drawing of Homestead feeder.

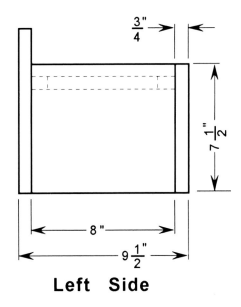

Left Side

Drawing of Homestead feeder.

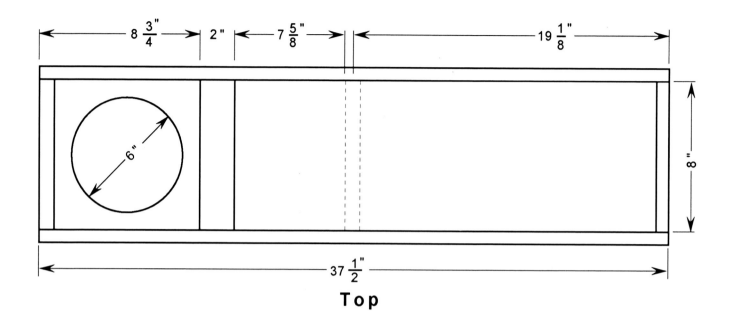

Top

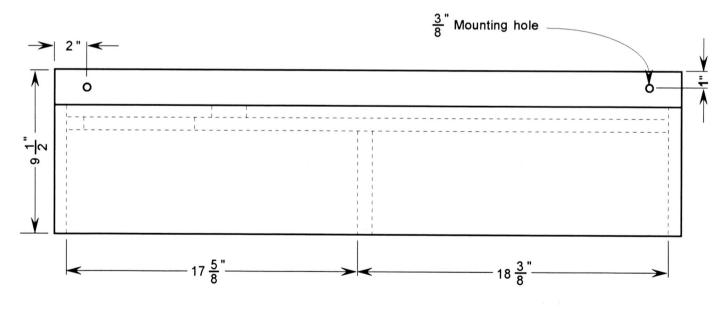

$\frac{3}{8}$" Mounting hole

Front

STATELY MANSION MATERIALS LIST

Wood

¾"-Thick Exterior Plywood Siding

Number of Pieces	Width	Length	Part
1	10"	16½"	Floor

¾"-Thick Redwood, Cedar, etc.

Number of Pieces	Width	Length	Part
2	1½"	11½"	Front and Back
2	1½"	17¾"	Sides
4	1⅛"	7¾"	Columns
3	1⅛"	20¼"	Beams
6	1"	7½"	Rafters

¾"-Thick Oak

Number of Pieces	Width	Length	Part
2	1½"	5½"	Jar Holder Sides
1	¾"	5⁵⁄₁₆"	Jar Holder Back
1	3⅝"	4½"	Seed Diverter

Aluminum Sheet

Quantity	Width	Length	Gauge	Part
1	16½"	21"	19	Roof
1	5"	5"	16	Lid Support
1	2½"	5½"	16	Flow Lever

Miscellaneous Materials

Rivets

Quantity	Diameter	Length	Type of Finish
4	¹⁄₁₆"	¼"	Flathead Aluminum
1	⅛"	⁵⁄₁₆"	Flathead Aluminum

Eyebolts (each with 2 Washers and 2 Nuts)

Quantity	Diameter	Length	Finish
4	³⁄₁₆"	1½"	Galvanized

Nails

Quantity	Size	Length	Finish
1 lb.	2d	1¼"	Elect. Galvanized

Deck Screws

Quantity	Size	Length	Finish
8	#6	1½"	Galvanized
2	#6	¾"	Galvanized

Large-Diameter Glass Jar with Metal Lid

INSTRUCTIONS

1. Lay out all parts on the proper types of material.

2. Cut out the pieces to the dimensions shown on the plans. Be sure to cut the indentation where the rafter fits onto the outer beams.

3. Start at the floor and attach the front, back, and sides with glue and nails.

4. Assemble the oak jar holder. Use a pilot drill for each nail hole. You can make a pilot drill by cutting off the head of a finish nail. Glue the joints before nailing.

5. Test to see if the lid support slides into the slots easily. Adjust the fit, if necessary. The jar support should be assembled now.

6. Place the jar holder in its proper location, mark around its four corners, locate the middle of each corner, and drill a ³⁄₁₆" clearance hole in the center point. Remove the jar holder and mark pilot hole locations through the clearance holes. Drill these marks with a ³⁄₃₂" pilot drill or a finish nail. Replace the jar holder and screw it into place with four deck screws. If the screws are too tight, remove them and use a larger pilot drill.

7. Glue and nail the seed diverter in place. Use six ¾" brads.

8. Now, put a column in each corner; follow the same mounting procedure used with the jar holder.

9. Take the two outer beams and place them on the front and back of the base. Now, align them for proper overhang, mark the locations of the columns on the underside of the beams, put the beams on the columns, and glue and nail them in place.

10. Make a chamfer on the top edge of the center beam. This can be planed or cut with a table saw. Put the center beam next to a side beam and locate the outer edges of the columns. This is where the rafters are located. Measure between these two marks to find the location of the center of the middle rafter; also mark this location on the outer beams.

11. Glue and nail the rafters in place on the center beams.

12. Bend the roof to its proper angle and place it correctly on the rafters. Mark locations of the rafters. Turn the roof over and measure in 1" at each rafter mark. Draw a cross at the center of each rafter mark and the 1" mark. Drill a ³⁄₁₆" clearance hole through the cross. Countersink the center rafter holes on the top side to fit the #6, ¾"-long deck screws.

13. Place the roof back on the rafters and mark the holes on the rafters. Drill clearance holes through the outer rafters and pilot holes in the center rafters.

14. Screw the 1" deck screws into the center rafters. Put a washer over each eyebolt hole before inserting it into the hole. Add a washer over the other end of the eyebolt and put on the nuts.

Stately Mansion feeder.

Another view of Stately Mansion feeder.

Drawing of Stately Mansion feeder.

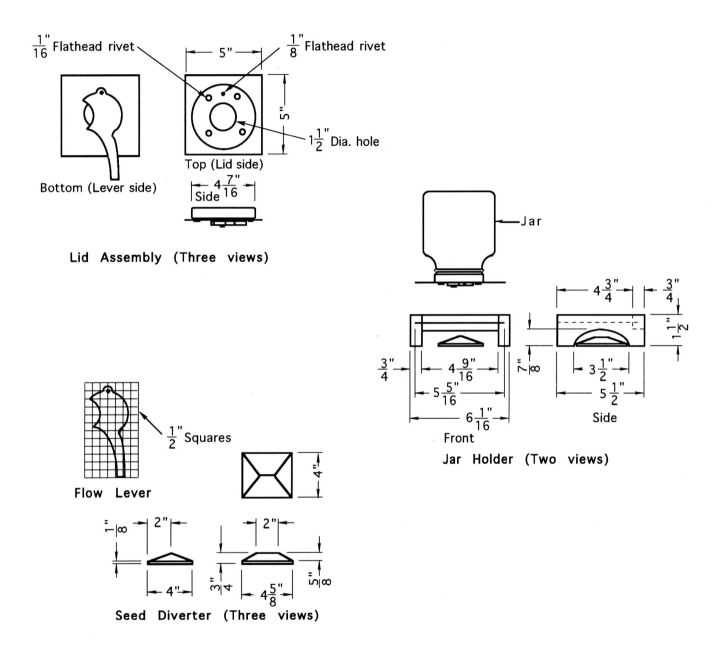

$\frac{1}{16}$" Flathead rivet

$\frac{1}{8}$" Flathead rivet

5"

5"

$1\frac{1}{2}$" Dia. hole

Top (Lid side)

Bottom (Lever side)

$4\frac{7}{16}$"

Side

Lid Assembly (Three views)

Jar

Jar Holder (Two views)

$4\frac{3}{4}$"

$\frac{3}{4}$"

$1\frac{1}{2}$"

$\frac{3}{4}$"

$4\frac{9}{16}$"

$3\frac{1}{2}$"

$5\frac{5}{16}$"

$5\frac{1}{2}$"

$\frac{7}{8}$"

$6\frac{1}{16}$"

Side

Front

$\frac{1}{2}$" Squares

Flow Lever

4"

$\frac{1}{8}$"

2"

2"

$\frac{3}{4}$"

$\frac{5}{8}$"

4"

$4\frac{5}{8}$"

Seed Diverter (Three views)

Drawing of Stately Mansion feeder.

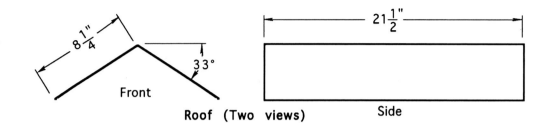

$8\frac{1}{4}$" $33°$

Front

Roof (Two views)

$21\frac{1}{2}$"

Side

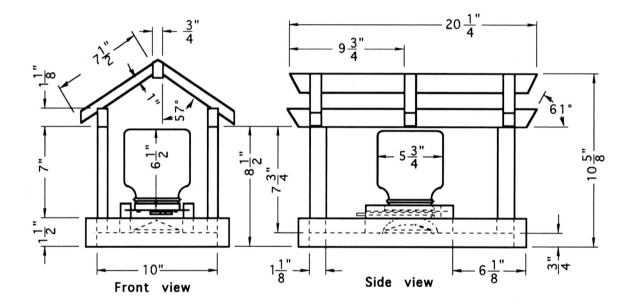

$\frac{3}{4}$" $7\frac{1}{2}$" $1\frac{1}{8}$" 1" $57°$ $6\frac{1}{2}$" 7" $1\frac{1}{2}$" 10"

Front view

$20\frac{1}{4}$" $9\frac{3}{4}$" $61°$ $5\frac{3}{4}$" $8\frac{1}{2}$" $7\frac{3}{4}$" $10\frac{5}{8}$" $1\frac{1}{8}$" $6\frac{1}{8}$" $\frac{3}{4}$"

Side view

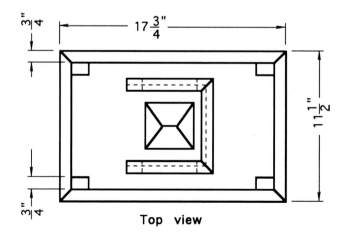

$\frac{3}{4}$" $17\frac{3}{4}$" $11\frac{1}{2}$" $\frac{3}{4}$"

Top view

WILL'S DOUGHNUT FEEDER MATERIALS LIST

Wood
¾"-Thick Redwood

Number of Pieces	Width	Length	Part
1	5⅞"	26"	Doughnut Holder

Miscellaneous Materials
Aluminum Sheet

Quantity	Diameter	Gauge	Part
1	17"	16 to 20	Shield

Hardware Cloth

Quantity	Mesh Size	Width	Length	Part
1	½"	16"	25"	Enclosure

Five Hardware Cloth Connectors

Screw Eye

Quantity	Diameter	Length	Part
1	³⁄₁₆"	3"	Screw-Eye Hanger

Staples

Quantity	Width	Length	Finish
10	³⁄₁₆"	½"	Galvanized

Rivets

Quantity	Diameter	Length	Material
3	¹⁄₁₆"	³⁄₁₆"	Aluminum

INSTRUCTIONS

1. Lay out the doughnut holder on the wood, and the shield on the aluminum sheet.

2. Cut the wood to size. Cut out the aluminum shield and drill the holes in it.

3. Drill pilot holes for a jigsaw or sabre saw on the wood.

4. Cut the doughnut holes to 4½".

5. Protect the wood with boiled linseed oil or prime and paint it.

6. Place the doughnut holder on wire mesh 2" from the right edge of the mesh. Fold up both sides of the mesh to get a proper fit.

7. Cut 2" up the left edge of the mesh.

8. Fold the edges down ½" to the inside to make the edges rigid.

9. Now, make the front (door) of the doughnut feeder by taking the remaining mesh and laying the doughnut holder on it ½" in from the right edge. Then cut the mesh ½" from the left edge.

10. Fold edges of this piece over ½" to the inside.

11. Cut the corner of the mesh so it can be folded inward as shown on the drawing.

12. Now, fold the bottom of the cover ½" inward. Then fold it another ½", to form a right angle.

13. Staple the wire mesh to the wood doughnut holder from top to bottom along the edges of the doughnut holder.

14. Secure the front of the edges of the doughnut holder with hardware cloth connectors, as shown on the drawing.

15. Make three small hooks as shown on the drawing. Attach the eye end to the top cover. This will pull the top over the edge for a tight fit.

16. Rivet the shield together with flathead rivets on the outside. Drill a ³⁄₁₆" hole on the top of the shield. Place the shield on the doughnut holder. Drill a pilot hole in the doughnut holder and screw in the screw eye.

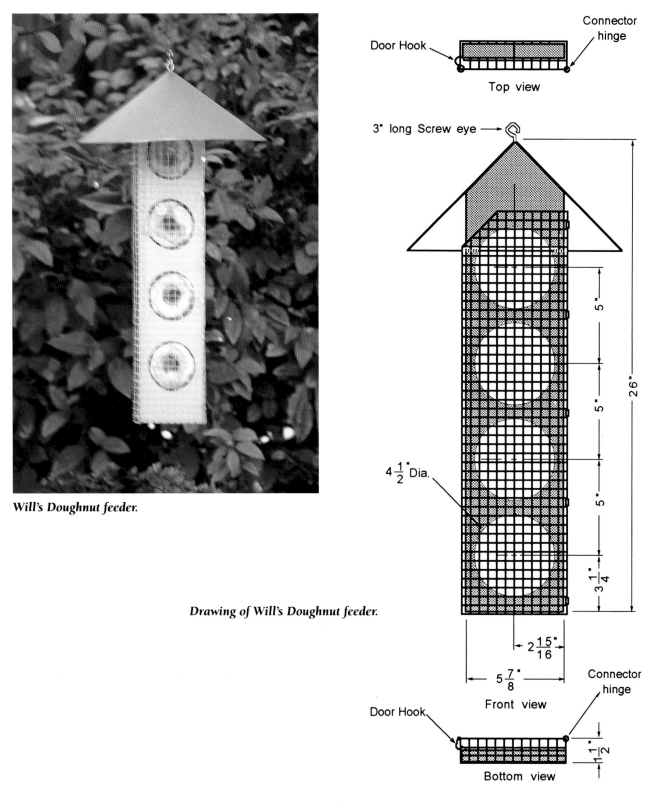

Will's Doughnut feeder.

Drawing of Will's Doughnut feeder.

Door Hook

Connector hinge

Top view

3" long Screw eye

$4\frac{1}{2}$" Dia.

5"

5"

5"

$3\frac{1}{4}$"

26"

$2\frac{15}{16}$"

$5\frac{7}{8}$"

Front view

Door Hook

Connector hinge

$1\frac{1}{2}$"

Bottom view

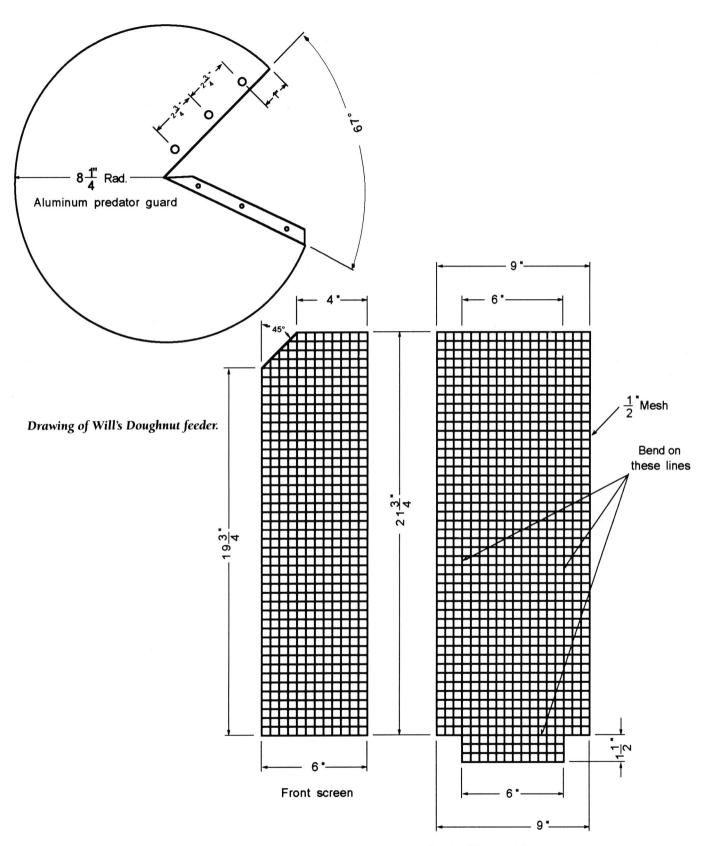

8 $\frac{1}{4}$" Rad.

Aluminum predator guard

67°

2 $\frac{3}{4}$"   2 $\frac{3}{4}$"   2 $\frac{3}{4}$"

Drawing of Will's Doughnut feeder.

45°

4"

9"

6"

$\frac{1}{2}$" Mesh

Bend on these lines

21 $\frac{3}{4}$"

19 $\frac{3}{4}$"

6"

Front screen

6"

9"

1 $\frac{1}{2}$"

Back, sides, and bottom screen

ASSEMBLAGES

Assemblage is a term used to describe unique feeders created from odds and ends. These projects can be built with items you've come across in your attic and cellar or with inexpensive bowls, trays, figurines, wooden knobs, etc., discovered in thrift shops, or at garage sales, flea markets, and rummage sales.

When assembling items, try to keep them in balanced proportions; usually the roof is larger than the bottom. Avoid bowls with sides more than two inches deep. Either turn your own spindles, banister knobs, and other fancy woodwork, or check at a large lumber supply store for ready-made ones. Another great source for fancy finials is a drapery department. (The ornaments used at the ends of drapery rods are ideal for spires.) Craft stores sell grab bags of hardwood turnings which can be incorporated into fabulous assemblages that look made-to-order.

To decorate an assemblage, use acrylic nonleaded paint with a water base. Paint only the roof and sides and not where the birdseed will be placed. Seal your completed project with a lacquer or urethane varnish spray. Read the directions to ensure that the ingredients aren't toxic.

Be sure to drill tiny drainage holes in the food tray and to rough up the edge of the bowl with sandpaper to give birds a better grip as they eat.

No two assemblages are alike. The directions for the following assemblages are not comprehensive, because the materials you use may vary from those given in the instructions.

BLUEBIRD OF HAPPINESS FEEDER

Supplies Needed

Two wooden salad bowls

One ¼″ threaded rod that is 12″ long

One wooden bird (or other objet d'art)

One screw eye

One ¼″ nut

Two hollow-turned wooden handles

One ¼″ acorn nut

Sandpaper

Assorted acrylic waterbase paints

Urethane varnish finish

Tools Needed

Hand drill and ⅛″ and ¼″ bits

Metal handsaw (to cut rod)

Paintbrush

Water dish

Directions

Arrange the items in order, from top to bottom, and assemble them. If you have a solid piece of wood such as a broom handle, use it instead of a metal rod and nuts for the center post. Attach it with screws. Try to keep the center post in the exact middle of the bowls. This can be tricky, because the great majority of bowls aren't symmetrical. Sand and paint the assemblage.

Bluebird of Paradise feeder.

COSMIC FANTASY FEEDER

Cosmic Fantasy feeder.

Supplies Needed

One balsa-wood moon cutout

One metal base from a nut bowl

One plastic flowerpot saucer

Two 9″-diameter plywood circles

Four 8¾″-long spindles

One banister knob

Assortment of hardwood turnings

Assortment of screws/nails

Aluminum ½″ and 2″ flashing strips

Decorative upholstery tacks

Acrylic paint

Wood glue and hot glue stick

One flange for pole mount

Tools Needed

Hand drill and ⅛″, ¼″, and ½″ bits

Screwdriver

Hammer

Paintbrush

Hot glue gun

Directions

Assemble the items from top to bottom and attach them with glue, nails, or screws as appropriate. When the assemblage is completed, sand and paint it.

ELEGANCE FEEDER

Supplies Needed

One drapery rod ornament

Two wooden salad bowls

One 1½″-diameter wooden closet rod

Assorted screws

One flange for pole mount

Sandpaper

Wood glue and hot glue stick

Nontoxic Paint

Tools Needed

Screwdriver

Saw

Hot glue gun

Hand drill and ⅛″ and ¼″ bits

Paintbrush

Directions

Assemble the items from top to bottom. Sand and paint the assemblage as needed. Attach the flange for the pole mount.

Elegance feeder.

PREDATOR GUARD MATERIALS LIST

Aluminum or Galvanized Sheet Metal

Quantity	Diameter	Gauge	Part
1	3′	16 to 20	Guard

Wood Blocks

Quantity	Thickness	Width	Length
3	1½″	1½″	5″

Aluminum Rivets

Quantity	Diameter		Length
3	¹⁄₁₆″		¼″

INSTRUCTIONS

1. Lay out the guard on the sheet metal.

2. Cut the guard to size. File or sand any rough edges.

3. Drill the four ¹⁄₁₆″ rivet holes 2″ apart.

4. Form the guard over a rounded object such as a baseball bat or a large pipe.

5. Place the guard on the pole to see if it will fit snugly once it is riveted together. Remember, check twice and cut once.

6. Rivet the ends of the guard together.

7. Slip the guard down over the pole to its desired location, mark the spot, raise the guard, nail in the blocks at your marks, drop the guard down over the blocks, and nail it in place.

The Predator Guard below the duck-nesting box prevents snakes and other swimming predators from gaining access.

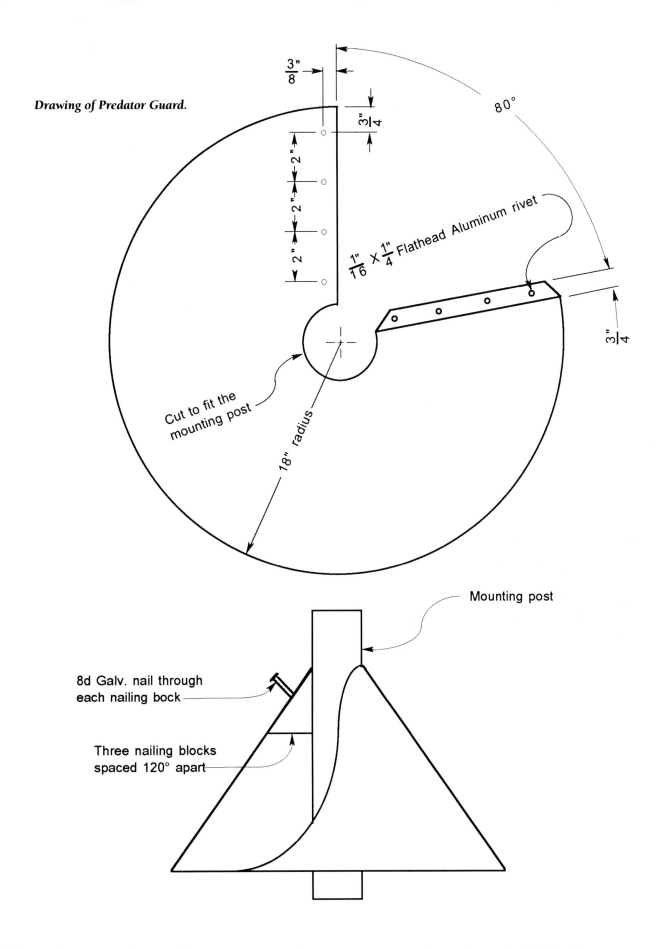

Drawing of Predator Guard.

$\frac{3"}{8}$

$\frac{3"}{4}$

80°

2" 2" 2" 2"

$\frac{1"}{16} \times \frac{1"}{4}$ Flathead Aluminum rivet

$\frac{3"}{4}$

Cut to fit the mounting post

18" radius

Mounting post

8d Galv. nail through each nailing bock

Three nailing blocks spaced 120° apart

GOURMET PECKINGS MATERIALS LIST

Hardware Cloth

Quantity	Mesh Size	Width	Length	Part
1	1½" square	54"	54"	Enclosure
	or 1" × 2".			

48 Hardware Cloth Connectors

INSTRUCTIONS

1. Cut in six squares from each corner of the mesh.

2. Bend all sides at right angles to the top of the mesh.

3. Use two hardware cloth connectors in each square. (See plan.)

4. Place the enclosure over food you want to protect from large birds and other predators.

Gourmet Peckings prevents large birds from eating food dropped from the feeder onto the ground.

Drawing of Gourmet Peckings.

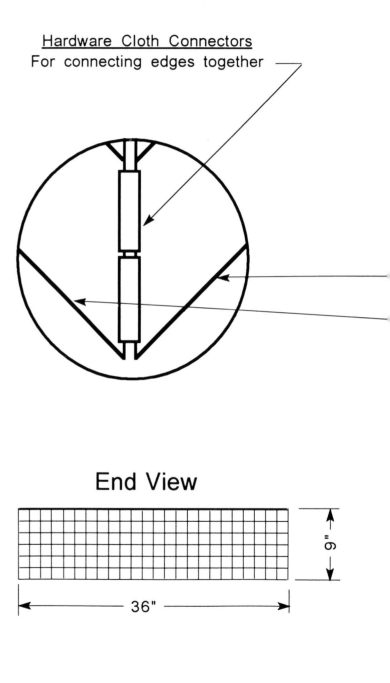

Hardware Cloth Connectors
For connecting edges together

End View

9"

36"

Top View

1 $\frac{1}{2}$" Mesh
(Squares)

54"

54"

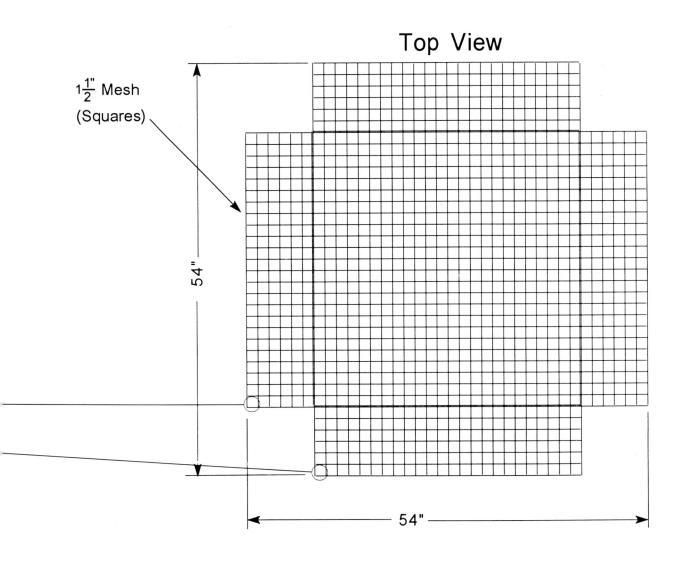

Side View

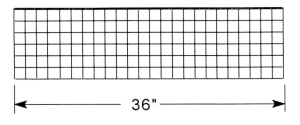

36"

6

Birdhouse Construction Factors

One bonus from feeding birds is that they may choose to nest nearby, or better yet, in a birdhouse in view from your window. Watching the comings and goings of nesting birds as they rear a hungry brood is a truly pleasurable activity.

When providing a suitable place for cavity-nesters, it is important to give some forethought as to which species you'd like to attract and, consequently, what kind of birdhouse is appropriate. Many people have been disappointed because their "cute" birdhouse hasn't been used. They are unaware there are reasons why the birds find such housing unsuitable. If you consider the following factors when building your

birdhouse, you will quite possibly find yourself being a landlord for the birds.

DESIGN

Make sure that the birdhouse has the correct dimensions for the species you intend to attract. For example, wrens need a birdhouse with a 4 × 4-inch floor space, a depth of 6 to 8 inches, and an entrance hole with a diameter of 1 inch. There are specific dimensions for each species. See the charts on pages 61–63 for examples of common species.

In addition to correct dimensions, a birdhouse should have one side that can be removed so it can be cleaned out and maintained after the nesting season is ended. A secure latch is essential, to deter predators. It's necessary for the roof to overhang on all sides, to protect the interior from the elements. To aid ventilation, a slot or several holes should be located just below the roof line. Small holes should be placed in the corners of the floor for adequate drainage.

To help young birds take their first trip out of the house, make a foothold by attaching a screen, cutting grooves, or tacking strips of wood on the interior face just below the entrance hole. *Omit a perch.* This isn't needed and will only encourage sparrows and predators to visit or take up residency.

The most critical measurement is for the entry hole If it's too small, the desired species can't enter; if it's too big, undesirable species will take up residence or the nest will be vulnerable to predators. Placement of the height of the hole is important so that young birds can eventually get out, but aren't within reach of cats and other predators.

MATERIALS

Good materials are important. Wood has better insulation qualities than metal or plastic. The best choices of wood are ¾-inch-thick plywood, redwood, cedar, or cypress. This wood can be a bit expensive, but in the long run it will be more weather-resistant and not warp as easily as spruce or pine.

Wood can be sealed with several coats of nontoxic linseed oil. (*Warning: Do not use chemical preservatives or treated lumber.* These harm birds.) If painting is desired, used lead-free exterior paint on the exterior only. The entrance hole should not be painted, so birds can get a good foothold.

Assemble the pieces with wood glue at joints and galvanized or stainless-steel screws and nails.

PLACEMENT OF BIRDHOUSES

Birdhouses should be placed on poles that are at least six feet off the ground, to discourage cats. If a wooden post is used, cover it with metal or plastic to hamper climbing. A cone or collar of metal can also deter predators. Metal poles are also acceptable. Place the birdhouse away from trees or other launching pads for squirrels.

Birdhouses could also be suspended by chains under eaves or hung from tree limbs. A birdhouse can be attached directly to a tree, but it's at risk from climbing predators. Barn owl houses have been located both inside or outside a barn. Duck houses can be placed on posts in water.

If predators do manage to reach a birdhouse, they might try to enlarge the entry hole to gain access to eggs. This can be remedied by placing a piece of hardware cloth or wire mesh on the front of the birdhouse with a hole cut to the *exact* size of the entrance.

Check a field guide for more information on the nesting habits of the species you'd like to attract. Wildlife management agencies are also an excellent source of information.

Note the predator guard at the entrance of the birdhouse.

This pole-mounted box discourages predators.

Install birdhouses early, before migrating birds arrive and breeding begins. (The specific time of the year to install them will depend on the region you are living in.) Many species will establish territories before nesting season.

MAINTENANCE

As soon as the offspring have fledged (are at the stage where they are flying), clean out the birdhouse to remove any lice, mites, or parasites that are in the nesting material. Dispose of the nest, wash the interior thoroughly with water, and spray the interior with a 1% rotenone powder or a pyrethrin-based insecticide. (This insecticide breaks down quickly and will not harm birds.)

To help birds in their quest for nesting materials, place a mesh bag or wire basket filled with suitable materials in a conspicuous place for the birds to find. Fill the container with usable items such as small bits of string or yarn (three inches long), the hair removed from your hairbrush, lint from the clothes drier, cotton balls, thread, carrot tops, and soft fibre trimmings. Once birds discover this treasure chest of goodies, they'll visit often and utilize the materials for their nests.

One of the funniest sights is seeing a sparrow holding a pile of clothes-drier lint bigger than its head and hopping around the garden looking for more. Another amusing sight is a "picky" bird rummaging through the offerings one by one, only to find that the last thing in the basket is suitable.

Swallows will look for a source of mud to build their nests along the eaves of a house, bridge, or barn. Providing a muddy spot in the garden will ensure they take up residence nearby.

Make necessary repairs by checking to see if all nails and screws are tight. Paint or treat the birdhouse with boiled linseed oil if the wood is showing deterioration.

Either remove the birdhouse or place a cover over the entry hole to keep insects, mice, or squirrels from moving in for the winter.

NESTING MATERIALS

Springtime brings on the most unusual bird behavior. Suddenly, out of nowhere a hummingbird plunges with lightning speed in a death-defying path towards earth. At the last possible moment, this tiny bird makes a 180° turn and repeats the maneuver again. Warblers and finches are singing their hearts out from dawn to dusk. Pigeons suddenly begin turning in circles as they parade along the garden path, and males of all species become aggressive towards one another.

What's happening? It's mating season! The urge to attract the opposite sex is very strong, and bird behavior often becomes bizarre as each species goes through the ritual of finding a mate.

After the preliminaries of attracting a mate have subsided and pair bonds are established, it's time for the birds to find a suitable site for nesting. Hopefully, your

Nesting materials.

birdhouses will be considered by the cavity-nesting birds, and the plant cover in the garden will serve both tree- and ground-dwelling species. Males will often select several suitable sites and start construction of a nest, but the female has the final word and will only settle where she decides. Brush piles can serve several species, which consist of both ground and tree nesters.

Nests will be constructed of a wide variety of materials. Twigs, weeds, stems, vine tendrils, soft grasses, spiderwebs, tree bark fibres, pine needles, moss, mud, and leaves are a few natural materials chosen for nest construction. Man-made materials are often used, too. String, bits of yarn, fishing line, bits of paper, rope fibres, small pieces of plastic, packing materials, and cloth scraps are a few items found in nest construction. Animal fur and hair, feathers, and straw have also been found in nests.

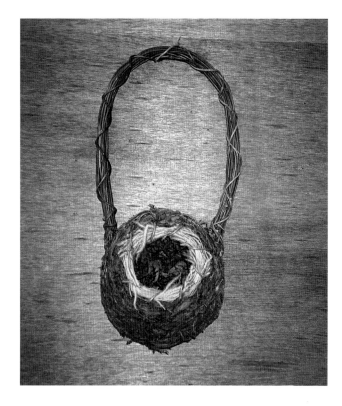

Man-made baskets serve as welcome ready-made nests.

DIMENSIONS FOR NESTING BOXES

Species	Floor of Cavity	Depth of Cavity	Diameter of Entrance	Entrance Height from Floor	Height Above Ground
Common Goldeneye	12″ × 12″	24″	4″–5″	20″–22″	4′–20′
Common Merganser	9″ × 9″ to 11″ × 11″	33″–40″	5″	28″–35″	8′–20′
Wood Duck	10″ × 18″	10″–20″	4″	12″–16″	10′–20′
Bufflehead	7″ × 7″	16″	2⅞″	13″–14″	10′–20′
Screech Owl	8″ × 8″	12″–15″	3″	9″–12″	10′–30′
Barn Owl	10″ × 18″	5″–18″	6″	4″	12′–18′
Barred Owl	12″ × 12″	20″–24″	6″	14″	15′–20′

Chart Continues on Following Page

Species	Floor of Cavity	Depth of Cavity	Diameter of Entrance	Entrance Height from Floor	Height Above Ground
Saw-whet Owl	6″ × 6″	10″–12″	2½″	8″–10″	12′–20′
Kestrel	8″ × 8″	12″–15″	3″	9″–12″	10′–30′
Hairy Woodpecker	6″ × 6″	12″–15″	1½″	9″–12″	12′–20′
Downy Woodpecker	4″ × 4″	12″–15″	1¼″	9″–12″	12′–20′
Redheaded Woodpecker	6″ × 6″	12″–15″	2″	9″–12″	12′–20′
Golden-Fronted Woodpecker	6″ × 6″	12″–15″	2″	9″–12″	12′–20′
Northern Flicker	7″ × 7″	16″–18″	2½″	14″–16″	6′–20′
Jackdaw	8″ × 8″	12″	6″	6″	10′–20′
Great-Crested Flycatcher	6″ × 6″	8″–10″	1⁹⁄₁₉″	6″–8″	8′–20′
Purple Martin	6″ × 6″	6″	2¼″	1″	10′–20′
Tree Swallow	5″ × 5″	6″–8″	1½″	4″–6″	4′–15′
Violet-Green Swallow	5″ × 5″	6″–8″	1½″	4″–6″	4′–15′
Chickadee	4″ × 4″	9″	1⅛″	7″	4′–15′
Titmouse	4″ × 4″	9″	1¼″	7″	5′–15′
Nuthatch	4″ × 4″	9″	1⅜″	7″	5′–15′
House Wren	4″ × 4″	6″–8″	1″–1¼″	4″–6″	4′–10′
Carolina Wren	4″ × 4″	6″–8″	1½″	4″–6″	5′–10′
Finch (House/Purple)	6″ × 6″	6″	2″	4″	8′–12′
Bewick's Wren	4″ × 4″	6″–8″	1¼″	4″–6″	5′–10′
Bluebird (Western/Eastern)	5″ × 5″	8″–12″	1½″	6″–10″	5′–10′

Dimensions for Nesting Shelves

Species	Sides	Depth of House	Size of Inside of House	Height Above Ground
Song Sparrow	All sides open	6″	6″ × 6″	1′–3′
Robin/Thrush	One or more sides open	8″	8″ × 8″	6′–15′
Phoebe	One or more sides open	6″	6″ × 6″	8′–12′
Barn Swallow	One or more sides open	6″	6″ × 6″	8′–12′

Precise measurements are important; if the diameter of the entry hole is larger than that needed, other, less desirable, species may usurp nest boxes and shelves. This might also put the nesting species in danger from attack by predators.

Birdhouse Plans

7

You've decided on the kind of bird you'd like to attract to the garden and you've picked out the design for the birdhouse. Before you begin, check the nest box dimensions chart in the previous chapter to determine that the dimensions of the birdhouse are compatible with the chosen bird. No matter how clever the design, if it doesn't fill the specific needs of the species you won't get a tenant. Use the exact measurements for the best results.

What type of finish should you put on your birdhouse? Birds aren't particular as to a color scheme. They try to be secretive when nesting and will be safer from predators if the birdhouses are of neutral colors. *Paint only the outside.* Leave the entry unpainted, to ensure a good foothold for the occupant. Seal the wood with several coats of boiled linseed oil. Don't use chemical preservatives! These can harm birds.

TYPE OF BIRD FOR EACH BIRDHOUSE

Birdhouse	Bird
1. Bob's Owl House	Barn Owl
2. Cherie's Beehive	Downy Woodpecker
3. Chi Chin Birdhouse	Tree Swallow
4. Martin's House	Purple Martin
5. Nesting Shelf	Robin
6. Peggy's Cove Birdhouse	Hairy Woodpecker
7. Pico Birdhouse	Bewick's Wren
8. Robedeau Round House	House Wren
9. Salt Box Charmer Birdhouse	Great-Crested Flycatcher
10. Sun/Moon Birdhouse	Nuthatch
11. Tahiti Getaway Birdhouse	Carolina Wren
12. Two-Gable Birdhouse	Violet-Green Swallow

BOB'S OWL HOUSE MATERIALS LIST

Wood
Any ¾"-Thick Exterior Plywood Siding

Number of Pieces	Width	Length	Part
2	23½"	17¾"	Sides
1	17½"	15¾"	Front
1	16⅜"	17¾"	Back
1	16⅜"	22"	Base (Bottom)
1	19½"	25"	Roof (Top)
2	3"	1½"	Mounting Poles

Fasteners
Nails

Quantity	Size	Length	Finish
1 lb.	5d	1¾"	Galvanized

Deck Screws

Quantity	Size	Length	Finish
24	#6	1½"	Galvanized

Carriage Bolts (with Washers and Nuts)

Quantity	Size	Length	Finish
4	⁵⁄₁₆"	2¾"	Galvanized

Eyebolts (with Washers and Nuts)

Quantity	Size	Length	Finish
4	⁵⁄₁₆"	3½"	Galvanized

INSTRUCTIONS

1. Lay out all parts on a plywood sheet or individual pieces of plywood.

2. Cut out all parts.

3. Cut drain slots in the base corners. Drill a pilot hole for a jigsaw, and make an entry hole. Drill vent holes. Sand the rough edges of the holes.

4. Attach the sides to the back with glue and nails.

5. Attach the front to the sides with glue and nails.

6. Attach the base to the front and sides with twelve #6 1½" deck screws equally spaced 3 on each side and end.

7. Place mounting poles on the back and drill the carriage bolt holes.

8. Put carriage bolts through the holes and add washers and nuts. Tighten the washers and nuts securely.

9. Add eyebolts through their pilot holes and put washers and nuts on them securely.

10. Attach the top with twelve #6 1½" deck screws. Equally space the screws, three to a side.

11. Finish the birdhouse with primer and three applications of latex house paint.

12. If mounting the birdhouse to a tree, use nylon rope or braided galvanized wire. Drill holes in the birdhouse to mount it on the surface of a barn.

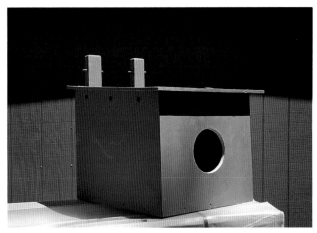

Bob's Owl House.

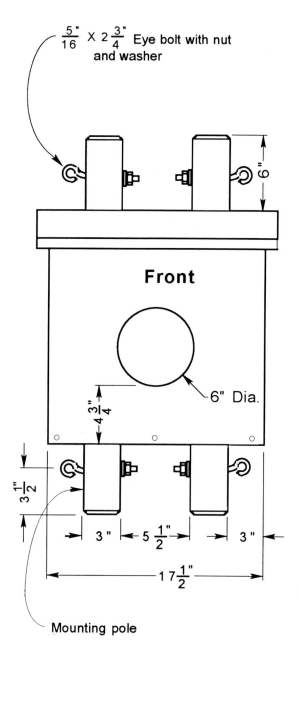

$\frac{5}{16}$" X $2\frac{3}{4}$" Eye bolt with nut and washer

Front

6"

6" Dia.

$4\frac{3}{4}$"

$3\frac{1}{2}$"

3 " 5$\frac{1}{2}$" 3 "

17$\frac{1}{2}$"

Mounting pole

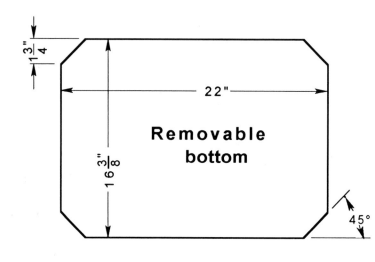

Another view of Bob's Owl House.

Drawing of Bob's Owl House.

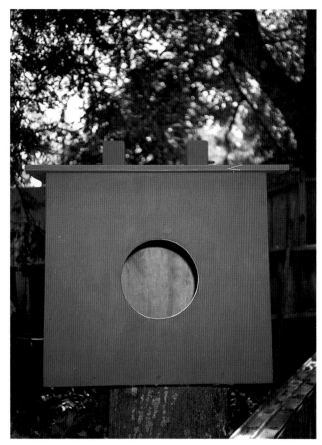

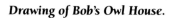

1$\frac{3}{4}$"

22"

Removable bottom

16$\frac{3}{8}$"

45°

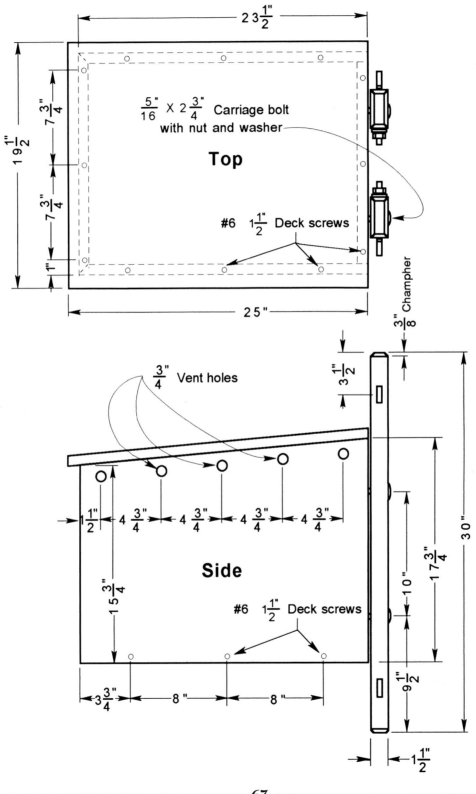

$\frac{5}{16}$" X $2\frac{3}{4}$" Carriage bolt with nut and washer

Top

#6 $1\frac{1}{2}$" Deck screws

$23\frac{1}{2}$"

$19\frac{1}{2}$"

$7\frac{3}{4}$"

$7\frac{3}{4}$"

1"

25"

$\frac{3}{4}$" Vent holes

$\frac{3}{8}$" Champher

$3\frac{1}{2}$"

Side

$1\frac{1}{2}$"

$4\frac{3}{4}$" $4\frac{3}{4}$" $4\frac{3}{4}$" $4\frac{3}{4}$"

$15\frac{3}{4}$"

#6 $1\frac{1}{2}$" Deck screws

$3\frac{3}{4}$"   8"   8"

30"

$17\frac{3}{4}$"

10"

$9\frac{1}{2}$"

$1\frac{1}{2}$"

CHERIE'S BEEHIVE MATERIALS LIST

Wood
Any ¾"- or 1"-Thick Redwood, Cedar, etc.

Number of Pieces	Diameter	Hole Size	Part
1	7¼"	No Hole	Top
1	6¾"	5½"	1st ring down
1	6¼"	5"	2nd ring down
1	5¾"	4½"	3rd ring down
1	5¼"	4"	4th ring down
1	4¾"	3½"	5th ring down
1	4¼"	3"	6th ring down
1	3¾"	2½"	7th ring down
1	3¼"	2"	8th ring down
1	2¾"	½"	Bottom (Base)

Fasteners
Nails

Quantity	Size	Length	Finish
½ lb.	3d	1¼"	Elect. Galvanized

Deck Screws

Quantity	Size	Length	Finish
6	#6	1½"	Galvanized

Eyebolt (with 2 Washers and 2 Nuts)

Quantity	Size	Length	Finish
1	³⁄₁₆"	1"	Galvanized

INSTRUCTIONS

1. Lay out all parts on a single sheet of 1" × 12" × 6' stock.

2. Cut out all parts.

3. Drill one ½" drain hole in the base and four pilot holes for #6 screws 90° apart and 1⅛" in from the edge.

4. Drill the ³⁄₁₆" center mounting hole and the four pilot holes for securing the top to the ring assembly.

5. Assemble the parts, starting with the 1st ring. Be sure to position the nails so they are not in line with the vent holes or the entry hole. There should be six ½" vent holes spaced 60° apart. Glue and nail the rings, spacing each ring ½" in on all edges.

6. Continue until all eight rings have been glued and nailed.

7. Secure the eyebolt to the top. Use one washer on the top, and the other on the inside. Use two nuts to lock the eyebolt in place.

8. Finish the birdhouse with three applications of boiled linseed oil or just leave the wood natural.

Cherie's Beehive.

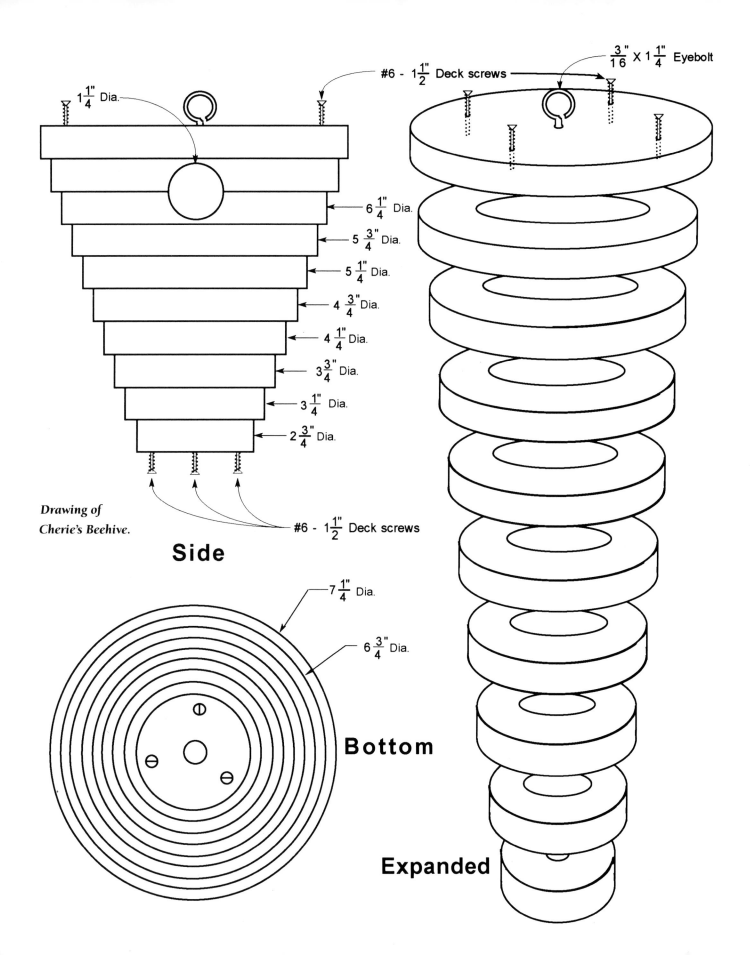

$1\frac{1}{4}$ " Dia.

#6 - $1\frac{1}{2}$ " Deck screws

$\frac{3}{16}$ " X $1\frac{1}{4}$ Eyebolt

$6\frac{1}{4}$ " Dia.

$5\frac{3}{4}$ " Dia.

$5\frac{1}{4}$ " Dia.

$4\frac{3}{4}$ " Dia.

$4\frac{1}{4}$ " Dia.

$3\frac{3}{4}$ " Dia.

$3\frac{1}{4}$ " Dia.

$2\frac{3}{4}$ " Dia.

Drawing of
Cherie's Beehive.

#6 - $1\frac{1}{2}$ " Deck screws

Side

$7\frac{1}{4}$ " Dia.

$6\frac{3}{4}$ " Dia.

Bottom

Expanded

CHI CHIN BIRDHOUSE MATERIALS LIST

Wood
Any ¾″-Thick Stock

Number of Pieces	Length	Width	Part
1	10″	10″	Top
12	7¼″	1½″	First Tier Section
12	6″	1½″	Second Tier Section
12	5¼″	1½″	Third Tier Section
1	5½″	5½″	Bottom

Fasteners

Nails

Quantity	Size	Length	Finish
½ lb.	5d	1¼″	Hot-Dipped Galvanized

Deck Screws

Quantity	Size	Length	Finish
12	#6	1½″	Galvanized

INSTRUCTIONS

1. Cut the pieces to the dimensions shown on the drawing.

2. Sand the exposed edges now, so you will not have to do it later when the birdhouse is assembled.

3. Start attaching the parts. Start with the first tier section. Lay out this section on the table. Stagger the middle layered section under the top section so that its sides overlap. (See the photo.) Glue and nail the top section to the middle section with 3d finish nails. Now,

glue and nail the third layer section to the top and middle sections to form one complete tier.

4. Take one piece of the second tier section and place it even with the outer edge of the first tier section and ½″ in from one side. Do not glue this part; nail it with only two nails. Locate the middle of the top section and the area where these two pieces join together. Drill your entry hole in this area.

5. Remove the nailed section and place it in its proper position. Glue and nail this tier together as you did the first tier.

6. Assemble the bottom tier as you did the other two.

7. Drill the drain and vent holes, as shown in the drawing.

8. Attach the bottom with four #6 1½″ deck screws.

9. Locate the middle of the top and drill a hole to

Chi Chin birdhouse.

accept a ³⁄₁₆″ eyebolt. Use washers on the top and on the inside of the top and put two nuts on the inside to lock it in place.

10. Attach the top with six #6 1½″ deck screws.

11. Finish the birdhouse with boiled linseed oil or prime and paint it as desired.

Layout of individual tier-section layer. Each is staggered as shown and overlapped for strength.

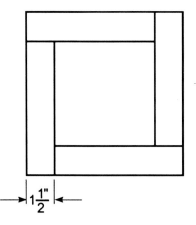

Drawing of Chi Chin birdhouse.

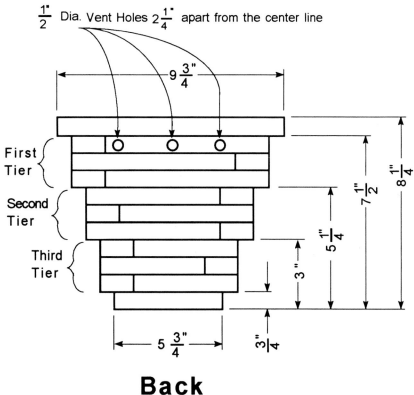

Back

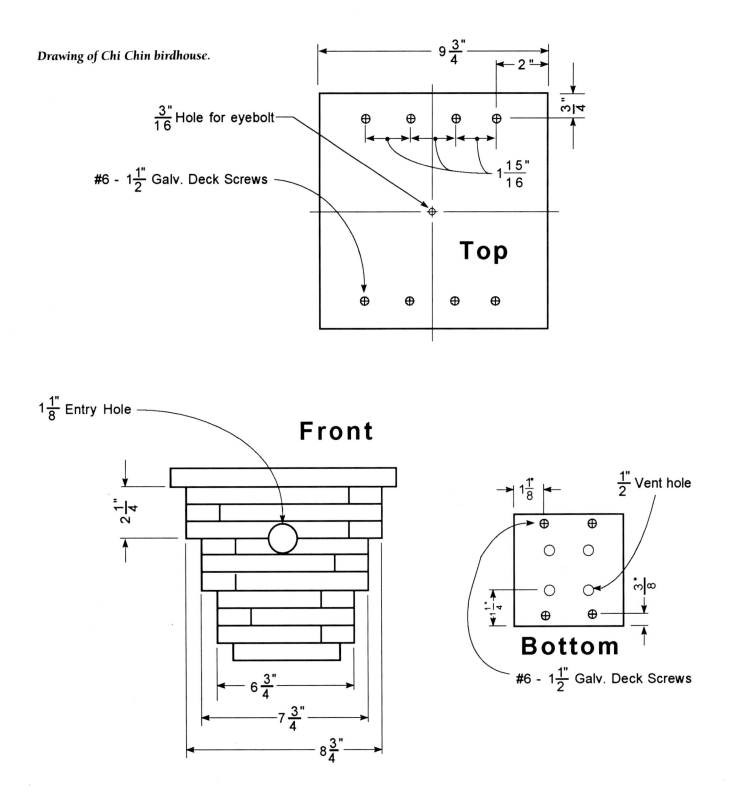

Drawing of Chi Chin birdhouse.

$\frac{3}{16}$" Hole for eyebolt

#6 - $1\frac{1}{2}$" Galv. Deck Screws

$9\frac{3}{4}$"

2 "

$\frac{3}{4}$"

$1\frac{15}{16}$"

Top

$1\frac{1}{8}$" Entry Hole

Front

$2\frac{1}{4}$"

$6\frac{3}{4}$"

$7\frac{3}{4}$"

$8\frac{3}{4}$"

$1\frac{1}{8}$"

$\frac{1}{2}$" Vent hole

$\frac{3}{8}$"

$1\frac{1}{4}$"

Bottom

#6 - $1\frac{1}{2}$" Galv. Deck Screws

72

MARTIN'S HOUSE MATERIALS LIST

Wood
Any ½"-Thick Exterior Plywood Siding

Number of Pieces	Width	Length	Part
2	25½"	16½"	Main Dividers I & II
4	12½"	16⅛"	Secondary Dividers
8	13"	5"	Dividers
8	10½"	8⅝"	Fronts
8	17¼"	11¼"	Roof Pieces
1	25½"	25½"	Base (Octagonal)

Fasteners
Nails

Quantity	Size	Length	Finish
1 lb.	2d	1¼"	Elect. Galvanized

Deck Screws

Quantity	Size	Length	Finish
8	#6	1"	Galvanized

Machine Screws (with Washers and Nuts)

Quantity	Size	Length	Finish
4	#10	1"	Galvanized

2" Galvanized Pipe Flange

2"-Diameter, 10'-Long Galvanized Pipe

Martin's House.

INSTRUCTIONS

1. Lay out all parts on a plywood panel or on individual sheets of plywood. When laying out the base, draw lines where the dividers and spacers meet the surface.

2. Cut out the pieces. The spacer and front pieces have a 35° angle on their tops. The fronts and spacers also have a 22½° angle on their sides. The dividers have a 22½° angle on both ends, which are cut from the centerline to each face. (Note the drawing.) The roof pieces have an 11° angle on their joining edges.

3. Cut the drain slots in the base as indicated in the drawing. Drill an entry hole, vent holes, and all other holes in the base. Sand the rough edges of the holes.

4. Assemble main divider II in the slot of main divider I; glue it along the seam, but not near the base.

5. Attach the main dividers to the base with deck screws. Do not glue them!

6. Assemble the secondary dividers. Glue the edges at the center where they meet the main dividers. Do not glue near the base. Screw the dividers to the base.

7. Install the spacers. Glue and nail them in place. Keep glue away from the base!

8. Attach the fronts to the dividers with glue and nails, taking care to keep glue off the base. You may have to plane the edges of the last front to get a perfect fit.

9. Attach the roof pieces with glue and nails. You may have to plane the last roof piece to obtain a good fit.

10. Finish the birdhouse with boiled linseed oil or prime and paint it as desired.

11. Mount the birdhouse on a pole by removing the base and nailing the birdhouse in place. For metal-pole mounting, use a screw-type flange to fit the pipe. Attach the flange with galvanized flathead machine screws, washers, and nuts.

Drawing of Martin's House.

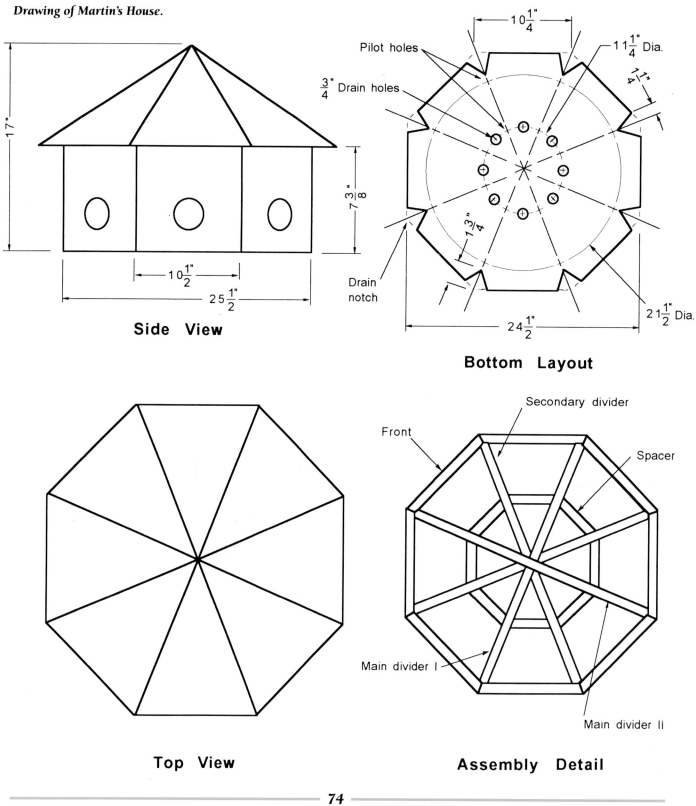

17"

$10\frac{1}{2}$"

$25\frac{1}{2}$"

$7\frac{3}{8}$"

Side View

$10\frac{1}{4}$"

Pilot holes

$11\frac{1}{4}$" Dia.

$1\frac{1}{4}$"

$\frac{3}{4}$" Drain holes

$1\frac{3}{4}$"

Drain notch

$24\frac{1}{2}$"

$21\frac{1}{2}$" Dia.

Bottom Layout

Top View

Secondary divider

Front

Spacer

Main divider I

Main divider II

Assembly Detail

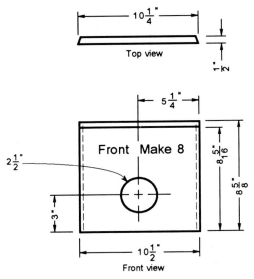

Front Section (Two views)

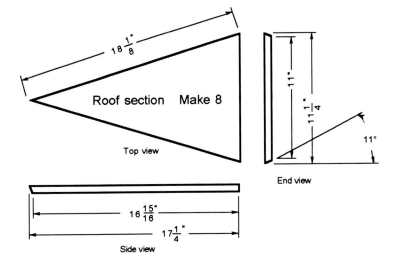

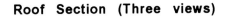

Roof Section (Three views)

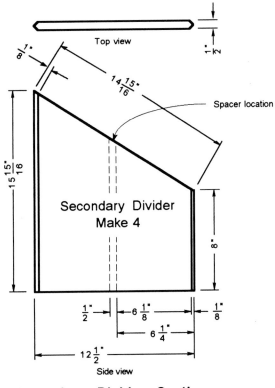

**Secondary Divider Section
(Two views)**

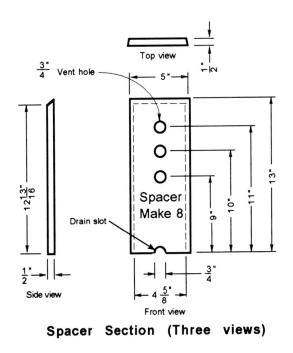

Spacer Section (Three views)

Drawing of Martin's House.

Main Divider Sections

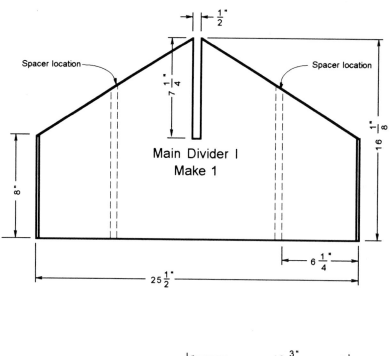

Spacer location

Spacer location

$\frac{1}{2}"$

$7\frac{1}{4}"$

$16\frac{1}{8}"$

8"

Main Divider I
Make 1

$6\frac{1}{4}"$

$25\frac{1}{2}"$

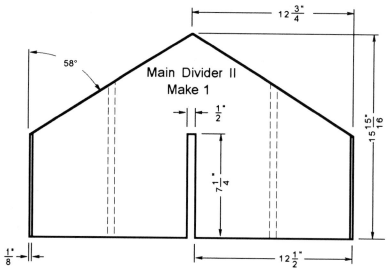

$12\frac{3}{4}"$

58°

Main Divider II
Make 1

$\frac{1}{2}"$

$15\frac{15}{16}"$

$7\frac{1}{4}"$

$\frac{1}{8}"$

$12\frac{1}{2}"$

NESTING SHELF MATERIALS LIST

Wood

¾″-Thick Exterior Plywood Siding

Number of Pieces	Width	Length	Part
1	8½″	7″	Back

½″-Thick Exterior Plywood Siding

Number of Pieces	Width	Length	Part
1	8½″	9⅝″	Top
1	6″	6¼″	Bottom

¾″-Thick Redwood, Cedar, etc.

Number of Pieces	Width	Length	Part
1	1½″	7½″	Front of Bottom
2	1½″	6¼″	Sides of Bottom

Hardwood Dowels

Quantity	Diameter	Length	Part
2	⅜″	7″	Support

Fasteners

Nails

Quantity	Size	Length	Finish
¼ lb.	5d	1¾″	Elect. Galvanized

INSTRUCTIONS

1. Lay out all parts on the wood.

2. Cut out all parts.

3. Attach the bottom to the back with glue and nails.

4. Attach the sides of the bottom and the front of the bottom to the bottom with glue and nails.

5. Drill ⅜″ holes in the middle of the sides of the bottom 2½″ from the back and at a 14° angle. (See the drawing.)

6. Drill ⅜″ holes 4″ from the back of the top and ⅞″ in from the edge at a 14° angle.

7. Insert dowels in the sides of the bottom.

8. Put the top in place over the dowels with glue and nail it to the back.

9. Finish the birdhouse with primer and paint it.

Nesting shelf.

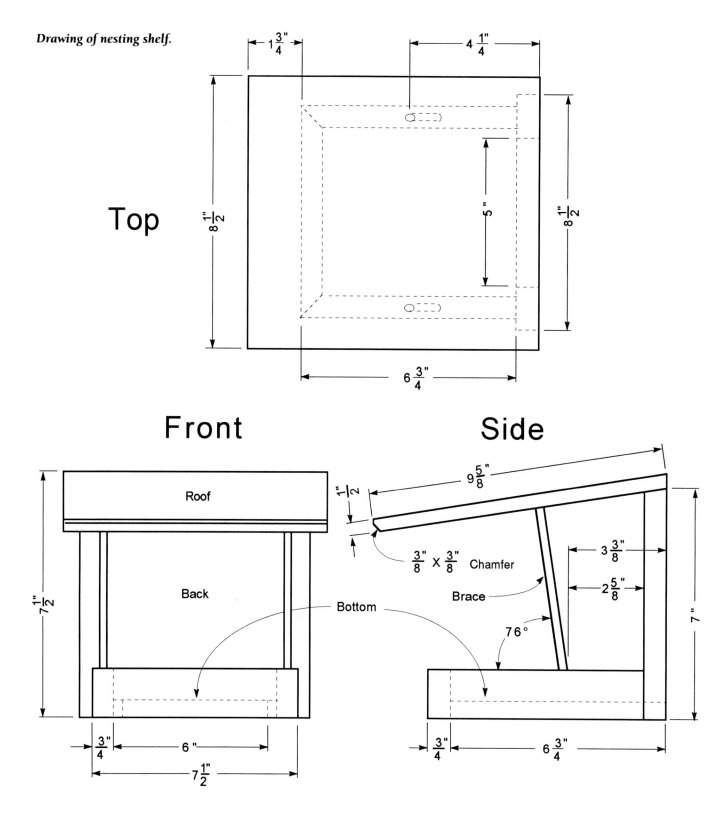

Drawing of nesting shelf.

Top

Front

Side

Roof

Back

Bottom

Brace

$\frac{3}{8}$" X $\frac{3}{8}$" Chamfer

PEGGY'S COVE BIRDHOUSE MATERIALS LIST

Wood

¾″-Thick Exterior Plywood Siding

Number of Pieces	Width	Length	Part
1	3³⁄₁₆″	3³⁄₁₆″	Part E (Octagon)
1	1⅜″	1⅜″	Part F (Octagon)
1	4¹⁵⁄₁₆″	4¹⁵⁄₁₆″	Part G (Octagon)
3	4¹⁄₁₆″	4¹⁄₁₆″	Part J (Octagon)
8	2⅞″	2″	Part A
8	2⅞″	3⅝″	Part B
8	2″	15¹¹⁄₁₆″	Part C
2	5⅝″	5⅝″	Part D
8	2¹¹⁄₁₆″	2⁹⁄₁₆″	Part H
8	2¹¹⁄₁₆″	2⁹⁄₁₆″	Part I
8	2″	1″	Part K
8	1¾″	3¾″	Part L

Hardwood Dowels

Quantity	Diameter	Length	Part
8	⅜″	4″	Part M (Stile)
8	¼″	2½″	Part N (Post)

Fasteners

Nails

Quantity	Size	Length	Finish
1 lb.	2d	1¼″	Elect. Galvanized

Deck Screws

Quantity	Size	Length	Finish
3	#6	1½″	Galvanized

INSTRUCTIONS

1. Lay out all parts on the wood.

2. Cut out the pieces. Parts A, B, C, H, and K have 22½° angles on their edges, while the pieces for Part L have 11° angles on their edges.

3. Assemble the pieces. Start at the bottom and work to the top. Glue and nail Parts A to both Parts D. Place Part E on Part D so that the spacing is the same on all edges. Glue and nail the pieces together.

4. Next, glue and nail all but one of Parts C to Parts E and F. Screw the last Part C to Parts E and F. This last Part C is the access port to the inside of the birdhouse.

5. Glue and nail Parts B to Parts C except for the one over the access port; use one screw to hold this one in place.

6. Glue and nail Part G to Part F and all Parts C except the removable one. Keep glue and nails away from this Part C.

7. Glue and nail all Parts H in place except for the one over the Part C that is removable. Screw it in place with one screw.

8. Drill the eight ¼″ holes in Part N ⅜″ deep and ½″ in from the corners.

9. Attach the eight Parts I to the two Parts J with glue and nails. Drill the eight ⅜″ holes in Parts I ⁵⁄₁₆″ in from the corners.

10. Put Parts K on the remaining Part J. Glue and nail them in place. Drill eight ⅜″ holes in Parts K ⁵⁄₁₆″ in from the corners.

11. Drill ¹⁄₁₆″ holes ⅜″ down from the ends of the ¼″ dowels (Parts N).

12. Glue in the eight ⅜″ dowels and six of the ¼″ dowels. The ¼″ dowels have their holes perpendicular to the joints in Parts H. Two of the ¼″ dowels are in the removable part of Part H. Do not put glue here.

13. Glue and nail Parts L to Parts K.

14. Assemble the windows and glue and nail them in place—opposite the removable pieces.

15. Drill an entry hole in the center of the middle window.

16. Finish the birdhouse by priming it with white primer and painting it white.

Drawing of Peggy's Cove birdhouse.

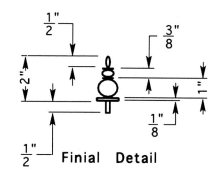

Finial Detail

Peggy's Cove birdhouse. See page 82 for assembly drawing.

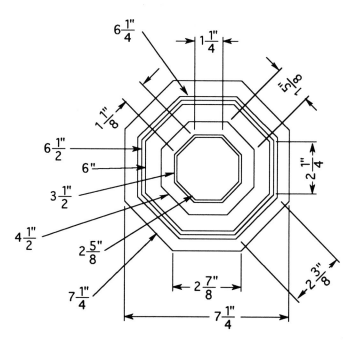

Top view of external octagonal dimensions.

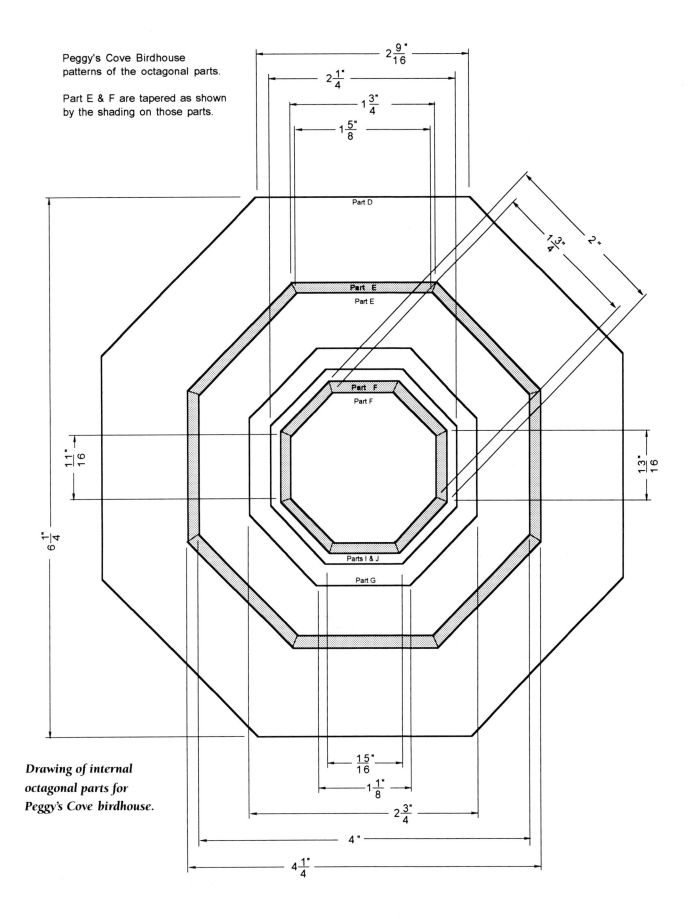

Peggy's Cove Birdhouse patterns of the octagonal parts.

Part E & F are tapered as shown by the shading on those parts.

$2\frac{9}{16}"$

$2\frac{1}{4}"$

$1\frac{3}{4}"$

$1\frac{5}{8}"$

$1\frac{3}{4}"$

$2"$

Part D

Part E

Part E

Part F

Part F

Parts I & J

Part G

$\frac{11}{16}"$

$\frac{13}{16}"$

$6\frac{1}{4}"$

$\frac{15}{16}"$

$1\frac{1}{8}"$

$2\frac{3}{4}"$

$4"$

$4\frac{1}{4}"$

Drawing of internal octagonal parts for Peggy's Cove birdhouse.

Drawing of Peggy's Cove birdhouse.

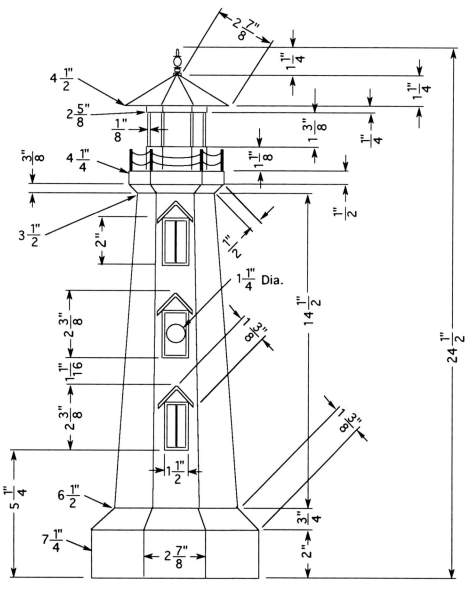

Front View

Drawing of Peggy's Cove birdhouse. See following page for additional views of these parts.

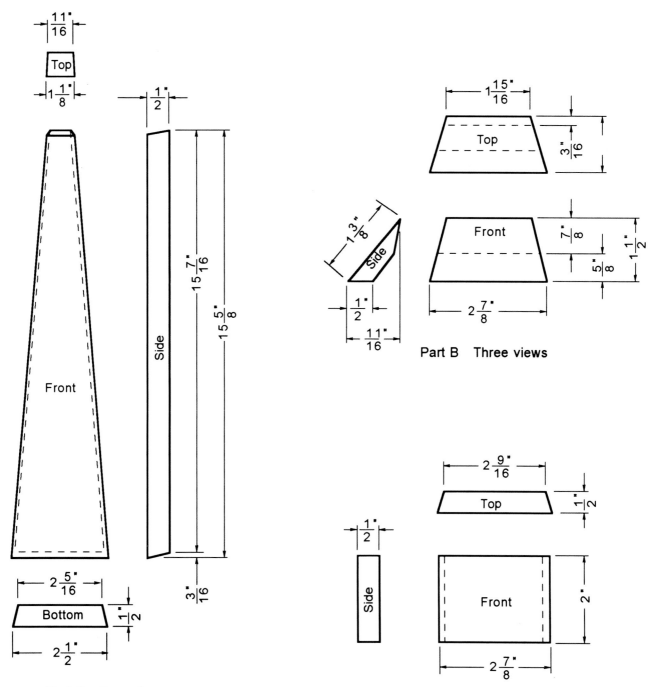

Part C   Four views

Part B   Three views

Part A   Three views

Drawing of Peggy's Cove birdhouse.

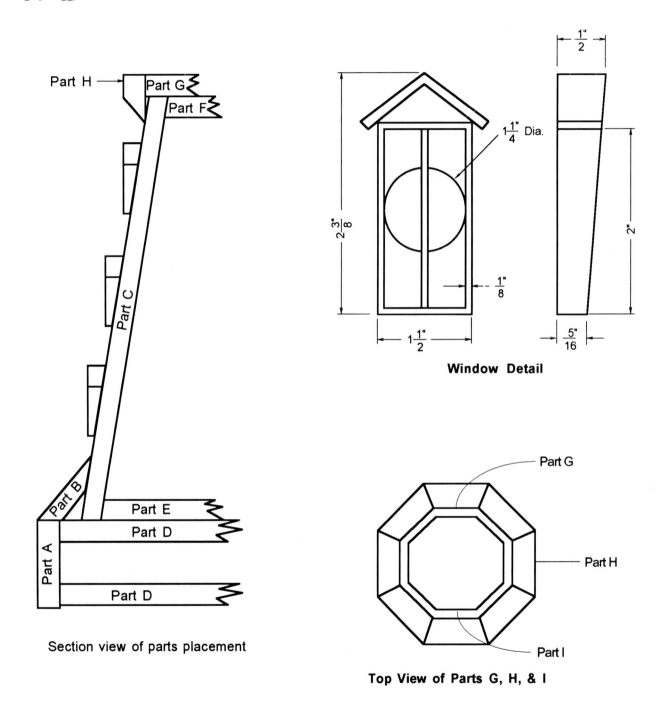

Part H → Part G
Part F

Part C

Part B

Part A

Part E

Part D

Part D

Section view of parts placement

1¼" Dia.

2⅜"

1⅛"

1½"

½"

2"

5⁄16"

Window Detail

Part G

Part H

Part I

Top View of Parts G, H, & I

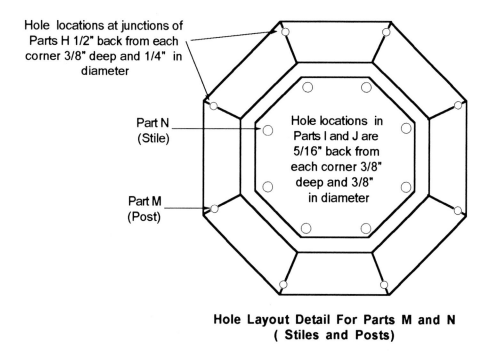

Hole locations at junctions of Parts H 1/2" back from each corner 3/8" deep and 1/4" in diameter

Part N (Stile)

Part M (Post)

Hole locations in Parts I and J are 5/16" back from each corner 3/8" deep and 3/8" in diameter

Hole Layout Detail For Parts M and N (Stiles and Posts)

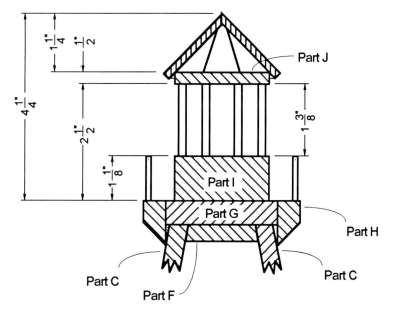

Part J

Part I

Part G

Part H

Part C

Part C

Part F

$1\frac{1}{4}$"

$\frac{1}{2}$"

$4\frac{1}{4}$"

$2\frac{1}{2}$"

$1\frac{1}{8}$"

$1\frac{3}{8}$"

Light Tower Assembly Detail

PICO BIRDHOUSE MATERIALS LIST

Wood

Any ½"-Thick Exterior Plywood Siding

Number of Pieces	Width	Length	Part
2	6¾"	6½"	Sides
1	4¾"	6⅝"	Front
1	4"	6"	Back
1	4"	4"	Base
1	6"	7¼"	Roof

Fasteners

Nails

Quantity	Size	Length	Finish
¼ lb.	2d	1"	Elect. Galvanized

Machine Screws

Quantity	Size	Length	Finish
4	#8-32	1"	Galvanized

Washers

Quantity	Size	Finish
4	#8	Galvanized

Nuts

Quantity	Size	Finish
4	#8-32	Galvanized

Deck Screws

Quantity	Size	Length	Finish
3	#6	1"	Galvanized

¾" Threaded Galvanized Pipe Flange

¾" Threaded Galvanized 10' Long Pipe

INSTRUCTIONS

1. Lay out all parts on a plywood sheet or individual pieces of plywood.

2. Cut out all parts.

3. Cut drain slots in the base corners. Drill an entry hole. Drill vent holes. Sand the rough edges of the holes.

4. Attach the sides to the back with glue and nails.

5. Attach the front to the sides with glue and nails.

6. Fasten the top to the sides and front with glue and nails.

7. Finish the birdhouse with boiled linseed oil or prime and paint it.

8. Secure a ¾" threaded flange to the base with galvanized flathead machine screws, washers, and nuts.

9. Fasten the base assembly in place with three screws (one on each side and one on the back).

10. Mount the birdhouse to a ¾" threaded metal pole with the threaded flange.

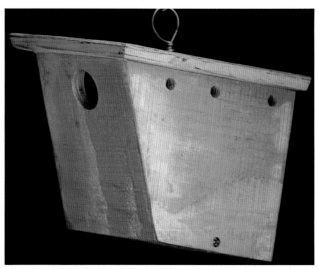

Pico birdhouse.

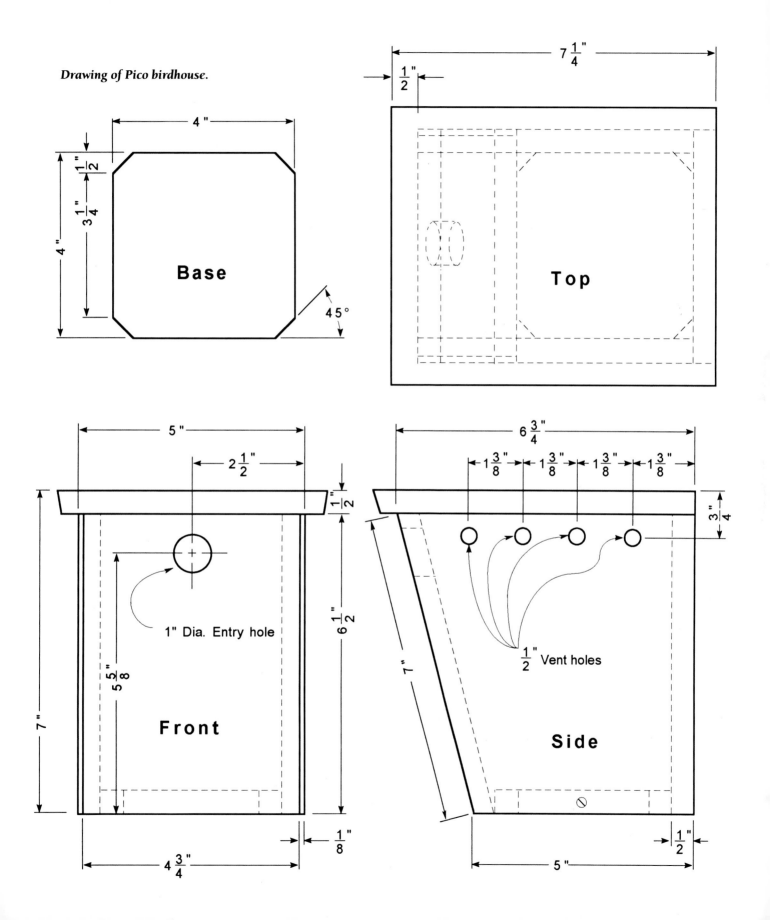

Drawing of Pico birdhouse.

4 "

1"/2

3 1/4 "

4 "

Base

4 5°

7 1/4 "

1/2

Top

5 "

2 1/2 "

1"/2

1" Dia. Entry hole

5 5/8 "

6 1/2 "

7 "

Front

4 3/4 "

1/8 "

6 3/4 "

1 3/8 " 1 3/8 " 1 3/8 " 1 3/8 "

3/4 "

1/2 " Vent holes

7 "

Side

1/2 "

5 "

THE ROBEDEAU ROUND HOUSE MATERIALS LIST

Wood
Any ¼"-Thick Exterior Plywood

Number of Pieces	Diameter	Part
1	3¹⁵⁄₁₆"	Top of Base
1	4⁷⁄₁₆"	Bottom of Base

Fasteners
Nails

Quantity	Type of	Length	Finish
4	Brad	⁷⁄₁₆"	Elect. Galvanized

Deck Screws

Quantity	Size	Length	Finish
4	#6	¾"	Galvanized

PVC Materials
Pipe

Quantity	Diameter	Length	Finish
1	4"	9"	Black

End Cap

Quantity	Diameter	Length	Finish
1	4"	Standard	White

Miscellaneous Materials (for Hanging from Tree)
Eyebolt with 2 Washers and 2 Nuts

Quantity	Size	Length	Finish
1	³⁄₁₆"	1"	Galvanized

Threaded Pipe Flange (for Pole- or Pipe-Mounting)

Quantity	Size	Diameter	Finish
1	¾"	3" to 4"	Galvanized

One Sheet 40-Grit Sanding Cloth

One Small Can PVC Cement

One 6-Ounce Tube Multi-Purpose Glue

INSTRUCTIONS

1. Cut 4"-diameter PVC pipe 9" long.

2. Cut a 1¼" ring off the pipe cap.

3. Glue and nail the two base pieces together with four ⁷⁄₁₆" brads so there is a ¼" shoulder all around. Position the brads away from the drain hole locations.

4. Drill and countersink the two holes in the shortened end cap and the 1¼" ring.

5. Drill the four ½" drain holes in the base 90° apart and 1⅞" from the middle. Drill the four ½" vent holes 1" down from the top edge and 1½" apart. Put these holes 180° away from the entry hole. Drill out the entry hole. Sand or scrape off burrs and rough areas.

6. Glue in the 40-grit sanding cloth from the base to the entry hole. Roughen the inside of the PVC pipe, so glue will adhere to the pipe and the cloth.

7. Assemble the parts, starting with the shortened end cap and the 1¼" ring. The ring can be glued in place, but the shortened end cap should be attached with screws.

8. If hanging the birdhouse from a tree, drill a ³⁄₁₆" hole in the middle of the cap and install an eyebolt with a washer and two nuts.

9. For pole-mounting, attach the flange on the base with four flathead galvanized machine screws, washers, and nuts.

10. Finish by wrapping colorful twine around the outside of the birdhouse; glue this in place.

Robedeau Round House.

Drawing of Robedeau Round House.

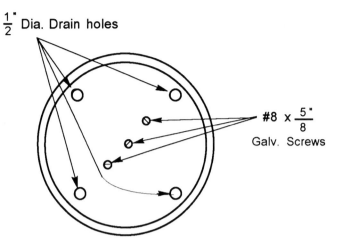

Bottom view (With Base)

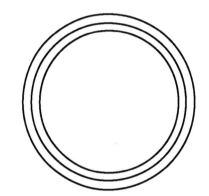

Bottom view (Without Base)

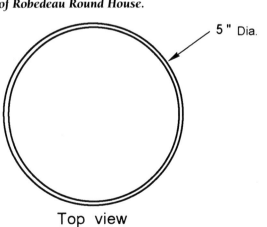

Top view

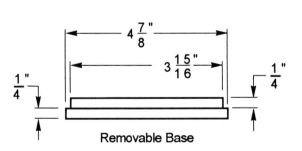

Removable Base

Drawing of Robedeau Round House.

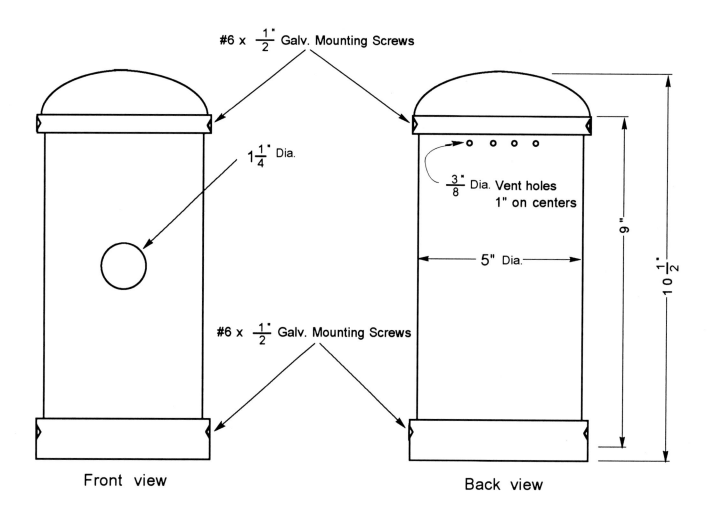

#6 x $\frac{1}{2}$" Galv. Mounting Screws

$1\frac{1}{4}$" Dia.

$\frac{3}{8}$" Dia. Vent holes
1" on centers

5" Dia.

9"

$10\frac{1}{2}$"

#6 x $\frac{1}{2}$" Galv. Mounting Screws

Front view

Back view

SALT BOX CHARMER BIRDHOUSE MATERIALS LIST

Wood

Any ½″-Thick Exterior Plywood Siding

Number of Pieces	Width	Length	Part
2	13¹³⁄₁₆″	12³⁄₁₆″	Right and Left Sides
1	11⅞″	5⁵⁄₁₆″	Back
1	11⅞″	8¹³⁄₁₆″	Front
1	11⅛″	8⁷⁄₁₆″	Divider
1	13⅜″	13¹⁄₁₆″	Left Roof
1	13⅜″	6½″	Right Roof
1	11⅛″	13⅞″	Bottom
2	2¹¹⁄₁₆″	2⁹⁄₁₆″	Chimney Front (Base)
2	2¹¹⁄₁₆″	2⁹⁄₁₆″	Chimney Side (Base)
1	3³⁄₁₆″	3³⁄₁₆″	Chimney Cap
4	½″	2¹¹⁄₁₆″	Chimney Top

Fasteners

Nails

Quantity	Size	Length	Finish
1 lb.	2d	1¼″	Elect. Galvanized

Deck Screws

Quantity	Size	Length	Finish
6	#6	1″	Galvanized

Flathead Machine Screws (with Nuts and Washers)

Quantity	Size	Length	Finish
4	#10	1″	Galvanized

2″ Galvanized Threaded Flange

2″ Diameter, 10′ Long Galvanized Threaded Pipe

INSTRUCTIONS

1. Lay out all parts on a plywood panel or on individual sheets of plywood.

2. Cut out the pieces. The front, back, and the divider have a ⁵⁄₁₆″ slant, and the roof pieces are cut at a 35° angle on each end. The front and back have rabbet joints at each edge.

3. If you want grooves, you can cut them with a router if desired, or they may be left off.

4. Drill an entry hole, vent holes, clearance holes, and pilot holes where indicated. Sand the rough edges of the holes.

5. Glue and nail the sides to the front and back. Position the divider in place and glue and nail it.

6. Place the left roof in place, aligning it for proper overhang on all sides, and glue and nail it with 2d finish nails. Adjust the right roof. You may have to plane it a little to get a perfect fit. Glue and nail it in place.

7. Now, assemble the chimney. It has a cap on it to prevent water from entering the birdhouse through the vent slot. Also, the front and back each have a vent hole.

8. Glue and nail the chimney in place.

9. Attach the bottom with six #6 deck screws where indicated on the front and back. If you want, place two screws on each side.

10. Finish the birdhouse with boiled linseed oil or prime and paint it as desired.

11. Mount the birdhouse on a pole by removing the base and nailing it in place. For metal pole mounting, use a screw-type flange that fits the pipe. Attach the flange with galvanized flathead machine screws, washers, and nuts.

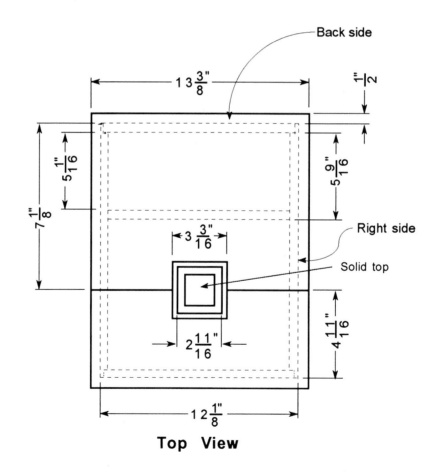

Salt Box Charmer birdhouse.

Drawing of Salt Box Charmer birdhouse.

Top View

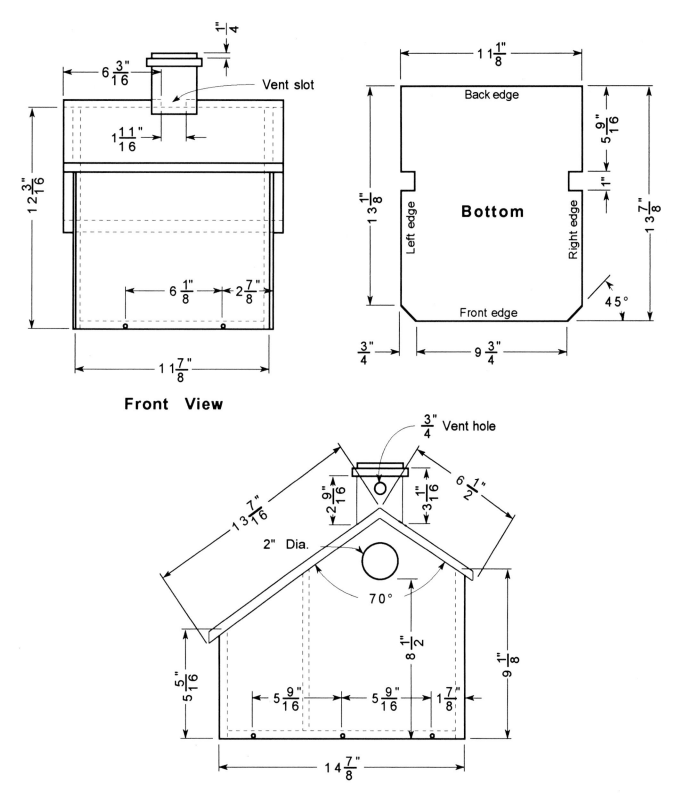

$\frac{1}{4}$"

Vent slot

$6\frac{3}{16}$"

$1\frac{11}{16}$"

$12\frac{3}{16}$"

$6\frac{1}{8}$" $2\frac{7}{8}$"

$11\frac{7}{8}$"

Front View

$11\frac{1}{8}$"

Back edge

$5\frac{9}{16}$"

1"

$1\frac{3}{8}$"

Bottom

Left edge

Right edge

Front edge

$45°$

$1\frac{3}{8}$"

$\frac{3}{4}$"

$9\frac{3}{4}$"

$\frac{3}{4}$" Vent hole

$2\frac{9}{16}$"

$3\frac{1}{16}$"

$6\frac{1}{2}$"

$13\frac{7}{16}$"

2" Dia.

$70°$

$8\frac{1}{2}$"

$9\frac{1}{8}$"

$5\frac{5}{16}$"

$5\frac{9}{16}$" $5\frac{9}{16}$" $1\frac{7}{8}$"

$14\frac{7}{8}$"

Left Side View

SUN/MOON BIRDHOUSE MATERIALS LIST

Wood
Any ¾″-Thick Stock (Redwood, Cedar, etc.)

Number of Pieces	Width	Length	Part
28	1″	4½″	Outside Edge Pieces
17	1″	4″	Inside Edge Pieces

½″-Thick Exterior Siding

Number of Pieces	Width	Length	
1	11″	12½″	Top Cover
1	15″	15″	Bottom (Base)

Fasteners
Nails

Quantity	Size	Length	Finish
1 lb.	5d	1¼″	Elect. Galvanized

Deck Screws

Quantity	Size	Length	Finish
1	#6	1″	Galvanized

Brass Hinges with Mounting Screws

Quantity	Size	Length	Finish
2	¾″	1½″	Brass

INSTRUCTIONS

1. Lay out the base on the wood to the dimensions indicated.

2. Cut the base.

3. Lay out the top as shown in the drawing: 7⅛″ for the left edge and 6⅝″ for the right edge.

4. Cut the bottom. (Note: The left section has a hinged clean-out door, so cut it before assembly. Also, there is a ⅜″ section that is removed for mounting the sides to the top and bottom.)

5. Cut 28 back and 17 front pieces as shown in the drawing. (The outside edge pieces are ½″ shorter than the inside edge pieces since their bottoms are fastened flush to the base.)

6. Before you nail and glue each back piece section together, trim it with a gouge to fit the contour of the base. Use the base as a support while nailing. Nails at vent holes, the entry hole, and drain holes should be carefully placed, to avoid difficulty in drilling these holes later.

7. Once the front and back are nailed and glued together, attach them to the base with nails and glue.

8. Use a rasp and wood file to obtain the proper shape, and then sand the assemblage.

9. Now, nail and glue the top in place. You will have to fit this part by chiselling out the excess material from the upper ledge of the front and back.

10. Drill the holes and sand the rough edges.

11. Finish the birdhouse with boiled linseed oil or prime and paint it.

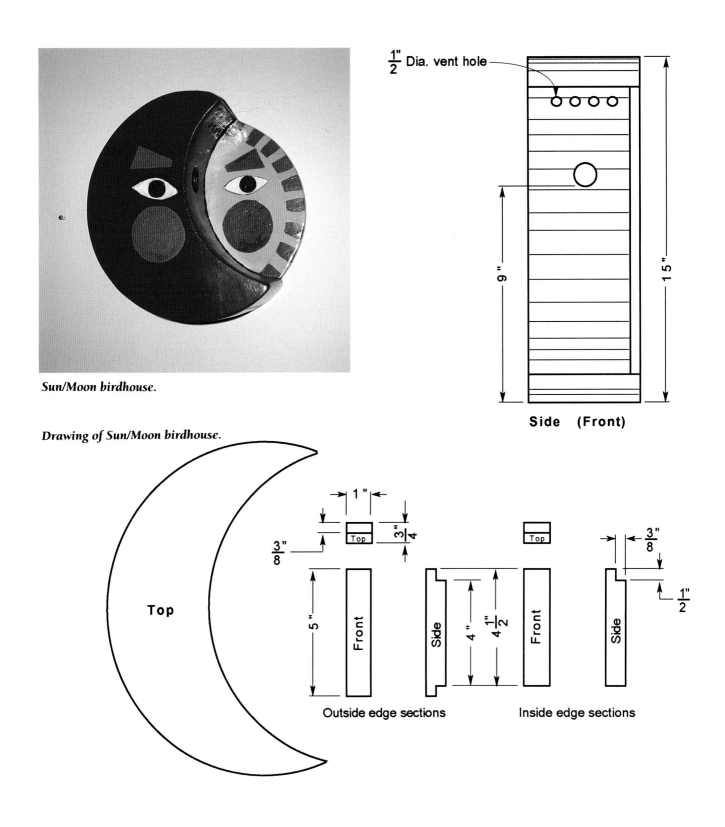

Sun/Moon birdhouse.

½" Dia. vent hole

Side (Front)

9 "

1 5 "

Drawing of Sun/Moon birdhouse.

Top

Top

1 "

3"/4

3"/8

5 "

Front

Side

4 "

4 1/2"

Front

Side

Top

3"/8

1"/2

Outside edge sections

Inside edge sections

Drawing of Sun/Moon birdhouse.

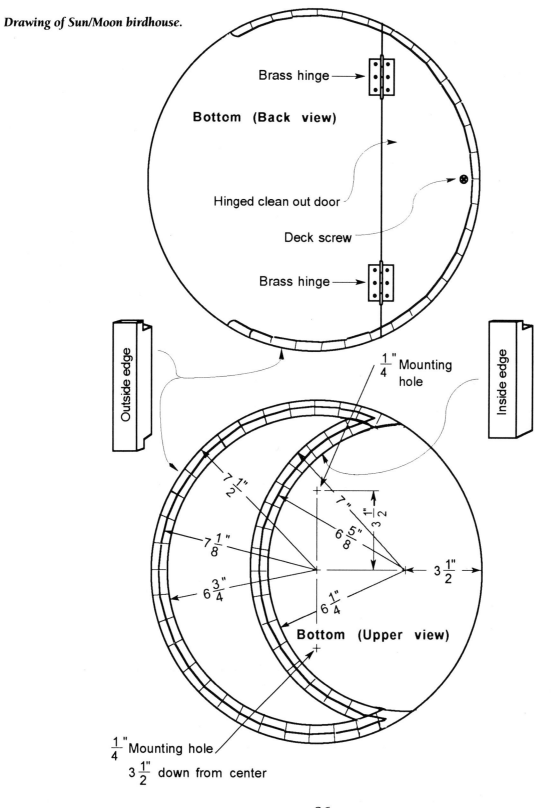

Brass hinge

Bottom (Back view)

Hinged clean out door

Deck screw

Brass hinge

Outside edge

Inside edge

$\frac{1}{4}$" Mounting hole

$7\frac{1}{2}$"

$7\frac{1}{8}$"

$6\frac{3}{4}$"

7"

$6\frac{5}{8}$"

$\frac{1}{3}\frac{1}{2}$"

$3\frac{1}{2}$

$6\frac{1}{4}$"

Bottom (Upper view)

$\frac{1}{4}$" Mounting hole
$3\frac{1}{2}$" down from center

TAHITIAN GETAWAY MATERIALS LIST

Wood

Any ½"-Thick Exterior Plywood

Number of Pieces	Diameter	Length	Part
8	2½"	7"	Top

Willow Branches or Grape Vines

Number of Pieces	Diameter	Length	Part
4	¼"	20"	Retainer Rings

Bark (Purchase from hardware store or cut from stump)

Number of Pieces	Width	Length	Part
1	6½"	18"	Sides
1	6"	6"	Base

Redwood Bark

Number of Pieces	Width	Length	Part
1	6½"	36"	Roof

Fasteners

Nails

Quantity	Type	Length	Finish
¼ lb.	Brad	¼"	Elect. Galvanized
¼ lb.	Brad	½"	Elect. Galvanized
10	Brad	1"	Elect. Galvanized

Hot Glue (with Hot Glue Gun)

Quantity	Diameter	Length	Finish
20 Sticks	¼"	4"	Clear

Miscellaneous Materials

Eyebolt

Quantity	Diameter	Length	Finish
1	¼"	1½"	Galvanized

INSTRUCTIONS

1. Shape the three rings to their proper sizes from willow branches or grapevines. Allow 3" for overlap.

2. Taper the ends of the rings so they can be joined together with glue and brads.

3. Cut the bark to size and glue and nail it to the proper rings. The bark may have a natural taper; if not, cut bark strips so they do have this taper.

4. Drill an entry hole as indicated on the drawing.

5. Nail the inside bottom ring in place with ½" brads.

6. Cut the bark base and hot glue it in place.

7. Drill four ½" drain holes in the base; space them 90° apart and near the inside ring.

8. Lay out the top pieces of roof. The edges are cut at 11° so they will fit nicely together.

9. Cut the roof pieces and assemble them with glue and nails.

10. Drill a hole in the top for an eyebolt and fasten it in place with washers and the two nuts as shown in the drawing.

11. Secure the top to the upper ring with 1" brads or galvanized wire.

12. Apply redwood bark, with hot glue, in shingle-like strips, starting at the lower edge of the roof. Be sure to overlap the bottom edge by about ¼″. Proceed around the top and work upwards for the second and subsequent layers. Put as many layers on as you feel necessary.

13. Finish the birdhouse with three applications of boiled linseed oil on the bark, but not on the redwood roof.

Tahitian Getaway.

Drawing of Tahitian Getaway.

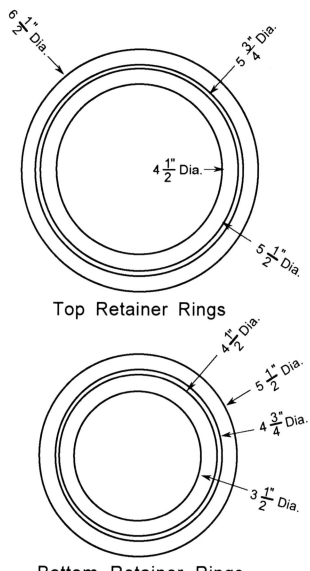

$6\frac{1}{2}$" Dia.

$5\frac{3}{4}$" Dia.

$4\frac{1}{2}$" Dia.

$5\frac{1}{2}$" Dia.

Top Retainer Rings

$4\frac{1}{2}$" Dia.

$5\frac{1}{2}$" Dia.

$4\frac{3}{4}$" Dia.

$3\frac{1}{2}$" Dia.

Bottom Retainer Rings

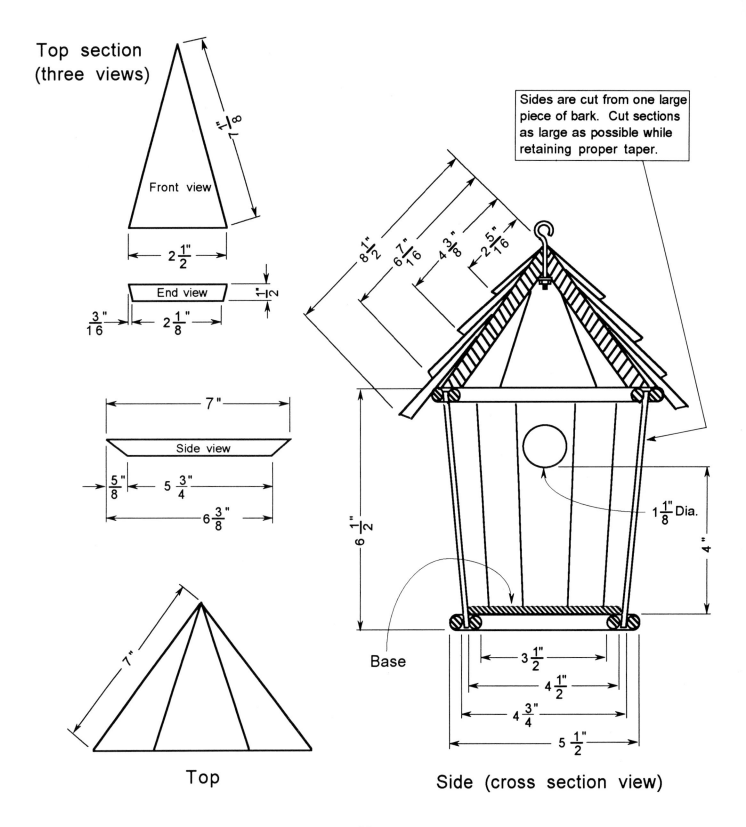

Top section
(three views)

Front view

$7\frac{1}{8}$"

$2\frac{1}{2}$"

End view

$\frac{1}{2}$"

$\frac{3}{16}$" $2\frac{1}{8}$"

7"

Side view

$\frac{5}{8}$" $5\frac{3}{4}$"

$6\frac{3}{8}$"

7"

Top

Sides are cut from one large
piece of bark. Cut sections
as large as possible while
retaining proper taper.

$8\frac{1}{2}$"

$6\frac{7}{16}$"

$4\frac{3}{8}$"

$2\frac{5}{16}$"

$1\frac{1}{8}$" Dia.

$6\frac{1}{2}$"

4"

Base

$3\frac{1}{2}$"

$4\frac{1}{2}$"

$4\frac{3}{4}$"

$5\frac{1}{2}$"

Side (cross section view)

THE TWO-GABLE BIRDHOUSE MATERIALS LIST

Wood

½″-Thick Oak Hardwood Flooring

Number of Pieces	Width	Length	Part
2	5″	7″	Sides
1	6″	9⅞″	Front
1	6″	10½″	Back
1	5″	5″	Base
2	5¾″	5⅜″	Large Roof
1	7″	2½″	Left Side of Small Roof
1	7″	1″	Right Side of Small Roof
2	⅞″	11⅝″	Right and Left Sides of Back
2	½″	11⅝″	Inside Spacers in Back
1	6″	11⅝″	Back of Back
1	¾″	4½″	Left Mounting Block
1	¾″	3¾″	Right Mounting Block
2	½″	11⅝″	Spacer

½″ Exterior Plywood

Number of Pieces	Width	Length	Part
1	3½″	24″	Mounting Board

Fasteners

Nails

Quantity	Size	Length	Finish
1 lb.	2d	1¼″	Elect. Galvanized

Deck Screws

Quantity	Size	Length	Finish
6	#6	1″	Galvanized

Carriage Bolts

Quantity	Diameter	Length	Finish
2	⅜″	7″	Galvanized

INSTRUCTIONS

1. Lay out all parts on the wood.

2. Cut out the pieces. The sides have bevelled tops, so cut them at the proper angle of 45°. Be sure to cut the tops at this angle also. The back of the back has rabbet joints on its edges. (See the drawing.)

3. Clean the grooves and tongues so glue will adhere to the surface if the wood is prefinished. Glue as many pieces together as needed. Use waterproof glue on all parts.

4. Drill drain holes in the base where indicated. Drill the entry hole, vent holes, and all other holes in the front. Countersink pilot holes to fit the screws. Sand the rough edges of the holes.

5. Attach the sides to the base with glue and nails. Drill pilot holes for all nails, to prevent splitting. Cut off the head of a finish nail, to use the nail as a pilot drill.

6. Screw the front to the sides and base. Do not use glue here. The front is removable. Now, nail the back to the sides and base.

7. Put the large roof pieces together with glue and nails. Next, glue and nail the mounting blocks to their inside positions on the left roof. Attach the large roof to the sides and backs with glue and nails. Do not glue or nail the large roof to the front. Just put in the top screw.

8. Assemble the slotted back with glue and nails. The mounting board fits in the slot, to make removal easy.

9. Finish the birdhouse with three applications of spar varnish. Sand lightly between coats with 200-grit sandpaper, wipe the varnish dust off, and apply the next coat of varnish. Repeat until the desired finish is obtained.

10. Mount the birdhouse on the pole by drilling a ½″ hole 11″ from the top. Cut a slot ½″ wide and 11″ long down to the ½″ hole. If using a portable saw, cut two slots and finish them with a handsaw. A chain saw will also do a good job here.

11. Drill mounting holes as shown in the drawing 2½″ down from the top edge and 6″ apart. Fasten the mounting board of the birdhouse in the slot of the pole with carriage bolts, washers, and nuts.

Drawing of Two-Gable birdhouse.

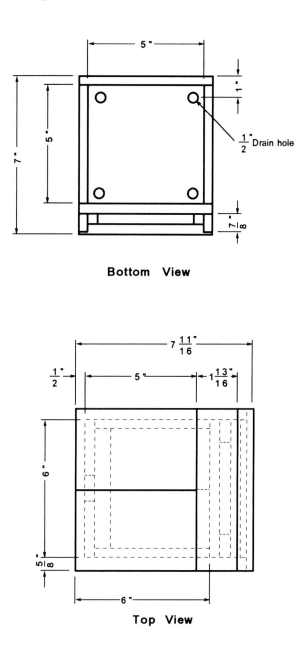

Bottom View

Top View

Two-Gable birdhouse.

Drawing of Two-Gable birdhouse.

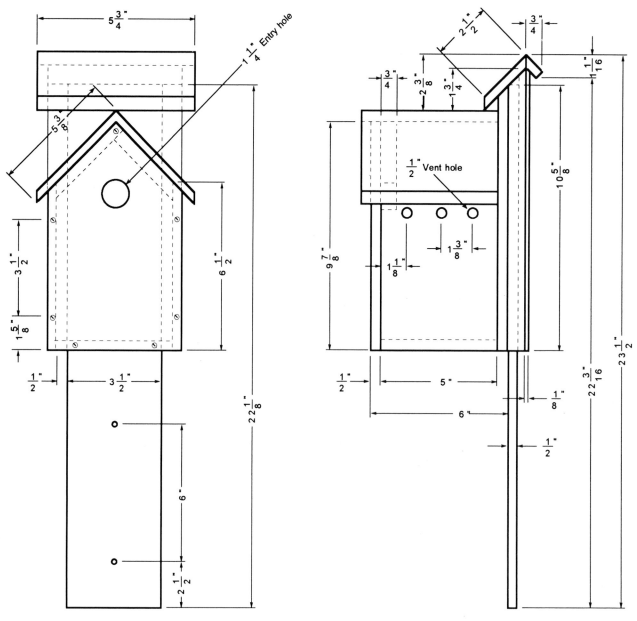

Front   View

Side   View

8

Birdbath
& Pool Plans

In addition to the plans that follow, consider using a combination of drippers and misters. Both use a small amount of water, but reap great rewards when it comes to luring birds to your garden. The sound of dripping water will attract birds from some distance away. An easy way to create a drip is to suspend a bucket of water above a birdbath and make a tiny hole in the bottom of the bucket, permitting a single drop to fall at short intervals.

INSTRUCTIONS

1. Select a piece of oak stump.

2. Cut the bottom so it is as flat as the top.

3. Lay out the shape of the bath liner on the stump end.

4. Rout out 2"-deep sections, starting at one edge and progressively working towards the other side. Do each section in four passes, increasing ½" in depth each time. Working from one side to the other will allow the router to have a firm base as you move across the stock.

5. Finish each section before starting the next; this way, you will not have to go back over any part.

6. Smooth the rough spots by hand.

7. Protect the birdbath with three coats of boiled linseed oil or leave wood natural.

8. Nail in the liner.

9. Fill the liner with water.

Nature's Birdbath.

Steps for constructing Nature's Birdbath.

1. Lay Out

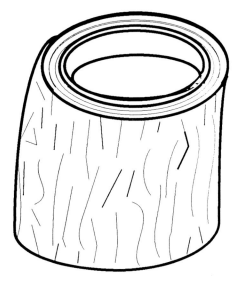

3. Put in Dish

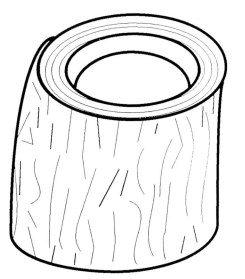

2. Rout Out

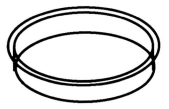

9" x 2" Plastic dish

DUGOUT BIRDBATH MATERIALS LIST

Wood
One Oak Y-Shaped Branch 12″ to 14″ in Diameter and 24″ Long

INSTRUCTIONS

1. Select a piece of oak with a Y-shaped branch.

2. Cut the bottom if necessary to make it lie flat.

3. Lay out a free-form shape with a 1½″ to 2″ wood gouge.

4. With a mallet and gouge, cut the basin 2½″ to 3″ deep. If you keep the gouge sharp, the cuts will be smooth and shiny.

5. Smooth the rough spots by hand.

6. Protect the birdbath with three coats of nontoxic water-based urethane.

7. Fill the birdbath with water.

Dugout Log Birdbath.

Steps for constructing Dugout Log Birdbath.

1. Lay Out

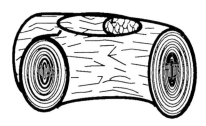

2. Gouge out

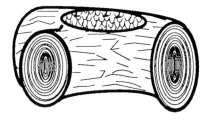

3. Finish

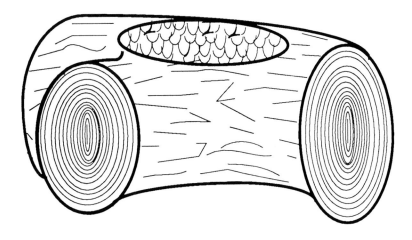

WILLOW BIRDBATH MATERIALS LIST

Wood

Willow Branches

Number of Pieces	Diameter	Length	Part
3	2½"	48"	Legs and perch
1	2¾"	30"	Leg

¾" Exterior Plywood

Number of Pieces	Diameter	Part
1	15"	Table

Terra-cotta Bowl

Quantity	Diameter	Depth	Part
1	13" or 14"	2"	Bath

Deck Screws

Quantity	Size	Length	Finish
5	#6	2½"	Galvanized
5	#6	2¾"	Galvanized
5	#6	3"	Galvanized

INSTRUCTIONS

1. Screw the branches together with #6 × 2½" to 3" deck screws. See the drawing for suggested placement and screw locations.

2. Place the round plywood in the top part of the branches and locate where the slots are to be cut. Lay out the size and depth of each cut.

3. Cut out the slots and again fit the plywood in the top part of the branches. When you have the right fit, sand the edges and screw the pieces into place.

4. Now, place the fourth leg on the assembly to give the bath stability. Use #6 × 3" deck screws.

5. Protect the birdbath with three coats of boiled linseed oil.

6. Place the terra-cotta bowl on the table and fill it with water.

Willow Birdbath.

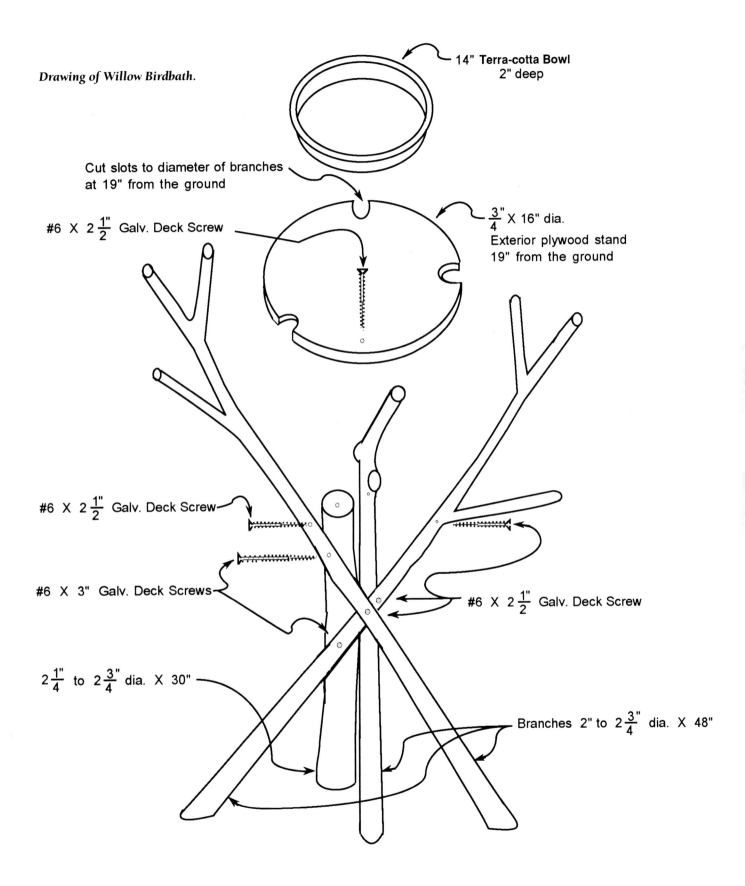

Drawing of Willow Birdbath.

14" **Terra-cotta Bowl**
2" deep

Cut slots to diameter of branches
at 19" from the ground

$\frac{3}{4}$" X 16" dia.
Exterior plywood stand
19" from the ground

#6 X 2$\frac{1}{2}$" Galv. Deck Screw

#6 X 2$\frac{1}{2}$" Galv. Deck Screw

#6 X 2$\frac{1}{2}$" Galv. Deck Screw

#6 X 3" Galv. Deck Screws

2$\frac{1}{4}$" to 2$\frac{3}{4}$" dia. X 30"

Branches 2" to 2$\frac{3}{4}$" dia. X 48"

Creating a Bird Sanctuary

sibility to continue providing a safe environment for birds to thrive in. This includes using alternatives to insecticides, chemical fertilizers, and fungicides, keeping unwanted guests (cats, squirrels, raccoons, etc.) away, and maintaining the landscape.

Encourage others to help the environment by providing gardens suitable for birds to thrive in. Every day will be full of enjoyment as the wonderful spectacle of nature is played out right outside your window.

These saucers with rocks provide water.

By providing food, water, and cover for birds in your garden, you have fulfilled the basic requirements of a bird sanctuary. There are several agencies that register gardens as sanctuaries and will certify your garden for a nominal fee. Ask your local bird-watching society, park department, utility district, and wildlife organizations for information on who registers gardens in your locality.

As the name implies, a bird sanctuary is a safe haven. Gardens near playgrounds or golf courses and other areas with a lot of activity would not be conducive to a good nesting habitat.

The owner of a certified bird sanctuary has a respon-

Let all who pass by know that you have created a bird sanctuary.

This bird station features a birdbath, a pinecone suet and seed feeder, and a seed feeder.

A source of shelter for birds.

Another source of water for birds.

A source of food for birds.

10

Alternatives to Chemicals

The urban gardener is faced with a dilemma: Should he control insects and weeds with chemicals, or use natural alternatives? Eliminating insects in a garden, both beneficial and bad ones, removes a food source for birds and, even worse, harms the garden. Since the objective is to attract birds to your garden, alternative ways to combat garden pests should be initiated. Using natural fertilizers and fungicides discourages weeds and fungus as well.

Here are a few tips on natural pest control:

1. For small infestations of insects, give plants a strong spray of water and remove the pests by hand.
2. Introduce to your garden beneficial insects such as ladybugs and lacewings that will eat offending insects.
3. Use less-toxic products such as insecticidal soaps, horticultural oil sprays, dehydrating dusts (diatoma-

ceous earth and silica gel), biological pesticides, and insect growth regulators.
4. Use boric acid ant baits, boiling water, or a pyrethrin solution to destroy ant nests. (Note: Because ants eat flea eggs and attack termites, the presence of ants in your garden may be an indication of a greater problem.)
5. Remove standing water if mosquitoes are a nuisance. Introduce mosquito fish to ponds.
6. When aphids appear, crush dense colonies at plant tips.
7. To rid plants of mites and aphids, use a solution of one tablespoon of dish soap, one cup of vegetable oil, and one cup of water. Mix these ingredients well and spray the mixture directly on the leaves. (Avoid using the mixture on vegetables in the cabbage family.)
8. Use a slow-release fertilizer such as fish emulsion rather than a nitrogen fertilizer, which produces fast, new growth and attracts aphids.
9. Bait snails and slugs with a saucer of stale beer at ground level. Remove the shells regularly.
10. Snails and slugs will not cross a copper barrier. Use a two-inch or wider strip of copper around raised plant beds.
11. Burn citronella candles when you are gathering outdoors. The smell from these candles will repel insects.
12. Consult with an agricultural specialist when insects get out of control. If you identify the pest, you can develop a nontoxic strategy to eliminate it.
13. Start a compost pile and/or worm bin to use as soil additives and fertilizers.
14. Organic soil amendments such as seaweed, fish emulsion, bone meal, peat moss, horn and hoof meal, blood meal, and manure are great alternatives to chemical fertilizers.
15. To control fungus, avoid overwatering your garden.
16. To control powdery mildew on rose leaves, spray both sides of the leaves with a solution of two tablespoons of mild liquid soap, ⅔ teaspoon of baking soda,

Birds love compost piles.

and one gallon of water.

17. Some plant diseases are treated with a copper solution (a Bordeaux mixture). Read the directions with care before using this solution.

18. Eliminate weeds by pulling them out by the roots.

19. Kill weeds before they mature and produce seeds.

20. Use woven black plastic fabric in flower beds to discourage weeds.

21. Cover bare areas with a heavy layer of mulch. Use eucalyptus mulch, if it is available. It has chemical properties that prevent seeds from germinating.

22. Reseed bare areas of lawns to discourage weeds from growing.

23. Keep lawns at least two inches deep, to discourage weed growth.

24. Encourage dense lawns by mowing them weekly.

SOURCES OF MORE INFORMATION

County agents, agriculture commissions, ecology organizations, organic gardening groups, health departments, pollution control agencies, and local libraries all provide sources of information on how to control insects.

There are fine books available. Here are a few titles:

Bradley, Fern M. *Rodale's Chemical-Free Yard & Garden: The Ultimate Authority on Successful Organic Gardening.* Rodale Press Inc., 1991.

Heloise. *Hints for a Healthy Planet.* New York: Putnam Publishing Group, 1990.

Klein, Hilary D., and Adrian Wenner. *Tiny Game Hunting: How to Trap & Kill the Pests in your House & Garden.* New York: Bantam Publishing Co., 1991.

Lifton, Bernice. *Bug Busters: Poison Free Pest Controls for House & Garden.* Avery Publishing Co., 1991.

Olkowski, William, et al. *Common-Sense Pest Control.* Taunton Publishing Co., Inc.

Finches perched on top of their nesting box.

Some Common Birds

Northern oriole.

American robin.

Great horned owl.

A golden-crowned sparrow feeding from a food dish.

American kestrel (sparrow hawk). The smallest of the falcon family, this bird has been known to visit large, open gardens in search of mice and small birds. Kestrels have the ability to hover above their prey. They tend to perch on poles or at the top of trees.

Western meadowlark.

Long-eared owl.

This chestnut-backed chickadee is enjoying a feast at a cone feeder made of suet and seeds.

Northern mockingbird in a persimmon tree.

Rock dove.

Great-tailed grackle.

Nuttall's woodpecker.

Dark-eyed junco.

Barn swallows.

WEIGHTS AND MEASURES

Unit	Abbreviation	Equivalents In Other Units of Same System	Metric Equivalent
WEIGHT			
		Avoirdupois	
ton			
short ton		20 short hundred weight, 2000 pounds	0.907 metric tons
long ton		20 long hundred weight, 2240 pounds	1.016 metric tons
hundred weight	cwt		
short hundred weight		100 pounds, 0.05 short tons	45.359 kilograms
long hundred weight		112 pounds, 0.05 long tons	50.802 kilograms
pound	lb t	16 ounces, 7000 grains	0.453 kilograms
ounce	oz *or* oz av	16 drams, 437.5 grains	28.349 grams
dram	dr *or* dr av	27.343 grains, 0.0625 ounces	1.771 grams
grain	gr	0.036 drams, 0.002285 ounces	0.0648 grams
		Troy	
pound	lb t	12 ounces, 240 pennyweight, 5760 grains	0.373 kilograms
ounce	oz t	20 pennyweight, 480 grains	31.103 grams
pennyweight	dwt *also* pwt	24 grains, 0.05 ounces	1.555 grams
grain	gr	0.042 pennyweight, 0.002083 ounces	0.0648 grams
		Apothecaries'	
pound	lb ap	12 ounces, 5760 grains	0.373 kilograms
ounce	oz ap	8 drams, 480 grains	31.103 grams
dram	dr ap	3 scruples, 60 grains	3.887 grams
scruple	s ap	20 grains, 0.333 drams	1.295 grams
grain	gr	0.05 scruples, 0.002083 ounces, 0.0166 drams	0.0648 grams
CAPACITY			
		U.S. Liquid Measure	
gallon	gal	4 quarts (2.31 cubic inches)	3.785 litres
quart	qt	2 pints (57.75 cubic inches)	0.946 litres
pint	pt	4 gills (28.875 cubic inches)	0.473 litres
gill	gi	4 fluidounces (7.218 cubic inches)	118.291 millilitres
fluidounce	fl oz	8 fluidrams (1.804 cubic inches)	29.573 millilitres
fluidram	fl dr	60 minims (0.225 cubic inches)	3.696 millilitres
minim	min	1/60 fluidram (0.003759 cubic inches)	0.061610 millilitres
		U.S. Dry Measure	
bushel	bu	4 pecks (2150.42 cubic inches)	35.238 litres
peck	pk	8 quarts (537.605 cubic inches)	8.809 litres
quart	qt	2 pints (67.200 cubic inches)	1.101 litres
pint	pt	1/2 quart (33.600 cubic inches)	0.550 litres
		British Imperial Liquid and Dry Measure	
bushel	bu	4 pecks (2219.36 cubic inches)	0.036 cubic metres
peck	pk	2 gallons (554.84 cubic inches)	0.009 cubic metres
gallon	gal	4 quarts (277.420 cubic inches)	4.545 litres
quart	qt	2 pints (69.355 cubic inches)	1.136 litres
pint	pt	4 gills (34.678 cubic inches)	568.26 cubic centimetres
gill	gi	5 fluidounces (8.669 cubic inches)	142.066 cubic centimetres
fluidounce	fl oz	8 fluidrams (1.7339 cubic inches)	28.416 cubic centimetres
fluidram	fl dr	60 minims (0.216734 cubic inches)	3.5516 cubic centimetres
minim	min	1/60 fluidram (0.003612 cubic inches)	0.059194 cubic centimetres
LENGTH			
mile	mi	5280 feet, 320 rods, 1760 yards	1.609 kilometres
rod	rd	5.50 yards, 16.5 feet	5.029 metres
yard	yd	3 feet, 36 inches	0.914 metres
foot	ft *or* '	12 inches, 0.333 yards	30.480 centimetres
inch	in *or* "	0.083 feet, 0.027 yards	2.540 centimetres
AREA			
square mile	sq mi *or* m^2	640 acres, 102,400 square rods	2,590 square kilometres
acre		4840 square yards, 43,560 square feet	0.405 hectares, 4047 square metres
square rod	sq rd *or* rd^2	30.25 square yards, 0.006 acres	25.293 square metres
square yard	sq yd *or* yd^2	1296 square inches, 9 square feet	0.836 square metres
square foot	sq ft *or* ft^2	144 square inches, 0.111 square yards	0.093 square metres
square inch	sq in *or* in^2	0.007 square feet, 0.00077 square yards	6.451 square centimetres

METRIC EQUIVALENTS CHART

Unit	Abbreviation		Approximate U.S. Equivalent

LENGTH

Unit	Abbreviation	*Number of Metres*	Approximate U.S. Equivalent
myriametre	mym	10,000	6.2 miles
kilometre	km	1000	0.62 mile
hectometre	hm	100	109.36 yards
dekametre	dam	10	32.81 feet
metre	m	1	39.37 inches
decimetre	dm	0.1	3.94 inches
centimetre	cm	0.01	0.39 inch
millimetre	mm	0.001	0.04 inch

AREA

Unit	Abbreviation	*Number of Square Metres*	Approximate U.S. Equivalent
square kilometre	sq km *or* km^2	1,000,000	0.3861 square miles
hectare	ha	10,000	2.47 acres
are	a	100	119.60 square yards
centare	ca		10.76 square feet
square centimetre	sq cm *or* cm^2	0.0001	0.155 square inch

VOLUME

Unit	Abbreviation	*Number of Cubic Metres*	Approximate U.S. Equivalent
dekastere	das	10	13.10 cubic yards
stere	s	1	1.31 cubic yards
decistere	ds	0.10	3.53 cubic feet
cubic centimetre	cu cm *or* cm^3 *also* cc	0.000001	0.061 cubic inch

CAPACITY

Unit	Abbreviation	*Number of Litres*	Cubic	Dry	Liquid
kilolitre	kl	1000	1.31 cubic yards		
hectolitre	hl	100	3.53 cubic feet	2.84 bushels	
dekalitre	dal	10	0.35 buic foot	1.14 pecks	2.64 gallons
litre	l	1	61.02 cubic inches	0.908 quart	1.057 quarts
decilitre	dl	0.10	6.1 cubic inches	0.18 pint	0.21 pint
centilitre	cl	0.01	0.6 cubic inch		0.338 fluidounce
millilitre	ml	0.001	0.06 cubic inch		0.27 fluidram

MASS AND WEIGHT

Unit	Abbreviation	*Number of Grains*	Approximate U.S. Equivalent
metric ton	MT *or* t	1,000,000	1.1 tons
quintal	q	100,000	220.46 pounds
kilogram	kg	1,000	2,2046 pounds
hectogram	hg	100	3.527 ounces
dekagram	dag	10	0.353 ounce
gram	g *or* gm	1	0.035 ounce
decigram	dg	0.10	1.543 grains
centigram	cg	0.01	0.154 grain
milligram	mg	0.001	0.015 grain

INDEX

Page Numbers in bold indicate color illustrations